CW01513269

The landscape of Greece is full of ghosts. Like the broken fragments of marble or the shards of pottery which turn up in the soil almost everywhere, the shades of the past have lingered long in this enchanted land. Almost every well, spring, cave, ravine, or mountain-top has its own story to tell.

Many concern the strange creatures known in Greek as *exotika*, or *xotika*. Some are benevolent, some are ambivalent or simply indifferent towards the human inhabitants of the land, while others are most definitely malevolent, bringing evil and suffering to all who encounter them.

Although in recent years the *xotika* have retreated before the advance of modern technology and the rational and sceptical spirit of the modern age, once the bright lights have been left behind, the traveller finds himself in a landscape at once alluring and threatening, where the fearful certainties of yesteryear seem more real than the superficial rationalisations of the present.

In *Haunted Greece* John L. Tomkinson takes a journey into the dark regions of the Hellenic folk memory. Here you will meet the fearful *stringles* who murder infants in their cots; beautiful nymphs who entice young men into insanity; the dead who climb out of their graves to prey upon friends and relatives; the mischievous demons who emerge from the Underworld during the twelve nights of Christmas; ox-headed serpents which haunt churches and fortell death; the rainbow-plumaged bird whose flight signals imminent catastrophe; and many even more terrible creatures. Some of them may have haunted the imagination of this most inventive people for more than three millennia.

Other books about Greece by John L. Tomkinson published by Anagnosis include:

Travellers' Greece: Memories of an Enchanted Land
Festive Greece: A Calendar of Tradition
Beyond Heaven and Earth: The Greek Church

Also, in the series *Greece Beyond the Guidebooks:*
Athens: The City
Athens: The Suburbs
Attica

Haunted Greece

Nymphs, Vampires
and other *Exotica*

John L. Tomkinson

Illustrated by
Maria Ine

Athens
Greece

Anagnosis
Harilaou Trikoupi 130
145 63 Kifissia
Athens, Greece
Website: www.anagnosis.gr

ISBN 960-88087-0-7

Photoset printed and bound by:
K. Pletsas - Z. Karadri O.E.
Harilaou Trikoupi 107
Athens
www.typografio.gr

Preface

Just as the *genre* of futuristic or "science" fiction may present us with the hopes and fears of an age and a people, so in the folk beliefs of our ancestors we may be able to gain some insight into their innermost aspirations, dreams, and nightmares; and so be enabled, in a limited fashion, to glimpse their world as they saw it. The folk heritage of the Greek people is a remarkably rich one, providing at the same time links to a justly celebrated past, and evidence of the continued fertility and inventiveness of the human imagination under very adverse conditions.

My aim has been to make available, in English, a small but representative sample of the rich variety of this tradition, gleaned both from collections made during the last century, when such beliefs were already beginning to fade, and also from the near-contemporary investigations of scientific anthropologists. As the beliefs recorded are no longer alive in the cities and towns among people who read books, and certainly among those who read books in English, I have referred to them consistently throughout in the past tense. This should by no means be taken to imply that all such traditions are now everywhere entirely extinct.

This work is offered in the belief that folk traditions provide us with insights into ways of looking at the landscape, ecology and human society which have largely passed from the collective consciousness, but which may yet have something to teach us.

John L. Tomkinson
Maroussi 2004.

Acknowledgements

Any survey of folk beliefs such as this is necessarily based upon the meticulous work of many field investigators, folklore collectors and scholars, working over more than a century. Detailed acknowledgements are made in the endnotes and bibliography. My thanks are also due to Marcus DeBaca, Despina Mouzaki, and to the librarians of the British School in Athens, the Gennadeion, and Athens College.

Contents

Haunted Landscape

The landscape of Greece is full of ghosts. Like the broken fragments of marble or shards of pottery which turn up in the soil almost everywhere, the shades of the past have lingered longer here than in most Western countries, although in increasingly attenuated form. Although Arnold Toynbee observed that "All human beings now alive have a heritage of equal length," he qualified this by pointing out that the Greeks are among those peoples which have preserved the longest memories of their past.[1]

The gods of the old formal state religions are no longer worshipped. Yet even they have not *entirely* vanished. Some live on in new guise, looking out at us from the icons of the Orthodox Church. Much more hardy, and much more resilient, were the spirits which inhabited nature, revered and feared by the country people, the original *pagani*, who gave us our word "pagan." The gods and spirits they feared and venerated probably predated many of the Olympians by many centuries, and *they* were by no means swept away by the imposition of Christian Orthodoxy.

Some of the places associated with them are still linked with their names. The mysterious "Old Panos" who was said to haunt the beautiful Cave of the Lamps, with its spring, its carved niches and its scattered shards of lamp offerings, on Mount Parnes, can be none other than the god Pan, to whom it was dedicated in ancient times.[2]

Among the many shades which haunt the magical landscape of Greece, the most numerous are the various types of non-human beings known collectively in Greek as *exotika* or *xotika*. Charles Stewart has isolated no fewer than thirty different such "species."[3]

Several generations have passed away since any significant section of the population has been bothered by such creatures in Western Europe. In England, a determined and successful campaign was waged against them by the puritan religious reformers of the sixteenth and early seventeenth centuries. Then the agricultural and industrial revolutions uprooted much of the population from its cultural roots, and forced them into the new industrial towns, delivering the *coup de grace*. Yet even in Britain, there is evidence that some of those who remained in the countryside, particularly on the "Celtic fringes," continued to live in an enchanted landscape for some while longer. In 1911, Jonathan Caredig Davies published his *Folk-lore of West and Mid-Wales*, which devoted no less than sixty pages to detailed accounts of beliefs about what the Greeks would call *xotika*, which may still have been current, at least as folk tales, in the second half of the nineteenth century.

In Greece, belief in the existence of *xotika* and other such creatures survived into the twentieth century. A friend of the author, now in early middle-age, and as far from traditional society by upbringing, education and temperament as it is possible to be, could recall his experiences as a child listening to the maid employed by his family, a girl from Arcadia, recite an apparently endless repertoire of stories about the various *xotika* which haunted her village, and about what happened to those who encountered them. An interviewee told researcher Dorothy Lee: "These things do happen. *Phantasmata* do exist. I was a policeman and had to go about at night. But when I went by haunted places, I always sang songs, and sometimes sacred chants."[4]

Unfortunately, it has always been difficult to get people to talk to strangers about such things. When belief was strong, people were simply afraid to talk about them. Theodore Bent recounted the following experience on Seriphos in the middle years of the nineteenth century:

"Seeing we were interested in this subject, the *demarchos* sent for an old woman popularly believed at Galene to be one hundred years old... Such a wrinkled piece of goods I never saw. She had on a white cap drawn forwards over her eyes, so that only the nose and chin could be seen *en profile*. Over this was a shawl tied round her chin; she had on a snuff-coloured short petticoat, stockings to match, a fur jacket, and over it a wide coat of brown Dutch carpet. She hobbled in, and seemed terrified of us, crossing herself lest we should cast on her the evil eye. She would not speak a word at first, in spite of the demarch's assurances that our intentions were peaceable.

"She almost shrieked when he spoke about Nereids, started up, and prepared to hobble away, but was persuaded to return. Again when the question was put she asserted, "I know nothing," shut her eyes, and groaned, and then, turning to our, by no means juvenile, host, she murmured, "My little boy, what are they going to do to me? "Thereupon everyone set to work to console her and stroke her, assuring her that the English meant no harm; so she at length told her tale in a low voice, which had to be translated to me from the dialect.

'Years ago Michael Kappazacharias was digging in his vineyard near St. Cyprian's Church.' Here she grew frightened again, and crossed herself violently before continuing, 'Well, it was a very calm, still day, when suddenly a whirlwind came and carried him to some distance; and as he was being borne along he felt the firm grip of the Nereids. Shortly afterwards he was found lying senseless, and carried in that state to the village . . .'"[5]

The reader of old travel books sometimes has the impression of an all-pervasive sense of fear among the country people, well conveyed in the following passage, written by the Earl of Caernarvon, about a journey he made in the Peloponnese in 1885:

"Once more we entered the wild rock scenery of the previous day, and traversed the Devil's Pass, where the muleteers maintained that belated travellers are attacked by demons. I asked what sort of demons. 'Nobody knew,' the muleteer replied, because no one passed after dark. 'No one for his soul's salvation would venture to go through that haunted pass after sunset, and few would dare to go alone in daylight. Wild and accursed moanings might be heard – the voice of fiends who simulated the sounds of birds or wild beasts.' One of our soldiers who, unlike the majority of our party, had been beyond the limits of the Maina, pretended to be incredulous, at which the muleteer was very angry, saying, 'Did not Demetrius, who was dead, appear, and throw a child into a pail in the court of the great tower and drown him; and did not some one else hear the mill grinding the corn at night though no mortal hand was near to move it?' As I was always ready to hear a legend, I looked grave, as if duly weighing the arguments on either side; upon which the soldier, seeing that I did not scoff at all notion of supernatural agency, as he supposed a Frank must do, dismissed the semblance of incredulity which he affected, and no longer insensible to the marvellous tales which he had pretended to despise, himself told strange and characteristic stories of the manner in which ghosts had come to their friends to urge them to take vengeance in Mainote fashion upon some member of a rival family."[6]

Writing of the late 1960s in certain settlements in Attica, only a few miles from Athens, Scott G. McNall reported that the villagers, relating stories of their experiences with *xotika,* would "cross themselves, look around, and keep moving their chairs. They are reluctant to use the word 'Devil' or 'Nereid,' and once they use it they say, 'You know who I mean. Them. The one I was just talking about.'"[7]

In practice, it is still very difficult to get people to commit themselves to a stranger. The reason is no longer usually fear, but shame. People do not want to be considered as backward "villagers", a term which has a bad odour in Greece, perhaps an indication of the recent liberation of most of the population from the still remembered hardships and restrictions of village life. Charles Stewart reported of Naxos during the 1980s, that information on *xotika* is now hard to come by. Country people are reluctant to admit to knowing anything about them. They realise that belief in *xotika* is associated with older and less educated people, and they consider that to admit to knowing anything about them at all is to appear backward and illiterate bumpkins.[8]

To the townspeople brought up during the Occupation and the Civil War, their life has often been a story of hard-won progress from village to metropolis, and from peasant farmer to civil servant, member of the professions, or *intelligensia.* Even to suggest that such a person might know something about *xotika* undermines their social pretensions, often a key element in their self-evaluation.

Nor is it a simple matter in any case to assess belief or disbelief. An individual does not necessarily simply "believe" or "disbelieve." Belief on any particular topic may be placed on a spectrum from unquestioned and unquestionable bedrock belief to contemptuous rejection. In between lies a range of beliefs which are liable to be rejected public, in the clear light of day, but which may return in private, when dusk falls, or when the traveller finds himself alone and far from human habitation. It is sometimes not very easy to say whether someone actually believes or does not believe. People may not even be able to answer that question honestly themselves. Dorothy Lee experienced such a range of attitudes in her research: ". . . it is from the Arcadians that I got the most vivid accounts of such beings, and for whom such experiences were most immediate. The accounts which I got from the Asia Minor Greeks were less personal, more in the nature of something heard and talked about, than of something felt."[9]

Intellectual Christianity likes to distinguish clearly between two mutually exclusive categories: the "natural" and the "supernatural". That this distinction is hardly applicable to Greek folk thought can be seen by an incident on travels of Lord Caernarvon: " . . . our Greeks were startled by a bird which flew across the road, and which they called *kira*. That bird . . . had once been a woman, who, deprived of all her kindred by some great calamity, retired to a solitary mountain to bewail her loss, and continued on the summit forty days, repeating in the sad monotony of grief the lamentation of the country, 'Ah me! ah me!' till at the expiration of that period she was changed by pitying Providence into a bird."[10]

Most of the *xotika* are essentially "natural," in that they are an integral part of this world and of the natural environment. Lee states, "these beings are often the very essence of nature."[11] They are weird and "unnatural" only in the sense that they may have powers, such as that of changing shape, which are beyond the normal. The term "paranormal" seems better suited to describe them. They are also natural rather than supernatural, because they are often vulnerable to attack through natural means, and although extremely long-lived, are mortal.

Since the boundary between the natural world and that of the *xotika* was never clearly conceived, some creatures have a highly ambiguous status. Lee points out: "The Arcadians made no clear distinction between what we would call fact and fiction, or history and folklore, in the stories which they told me. The accounts they gave of contact with non-human beings they referred to simply as *gegonata* (events) or *anecdota*."[12] Any unusual event will be treated in the same way as a story about an encounter with the *xotika*. A particularly large and potentially dangerous snake, for example, will be treated as *xotiko*, since it will inspire a response of awe and fear in those who encounter it, and since it will be dreaded by those who hear of it.

Popular Christianity, heavily influenced by Manichean dualism, seeks to divide the world into two mutually hostile camps: one representing "goodness", loyal to god and the saints, and another "evil", serving Satan and his cohorts. Although strictly unorthodox, and frequently combated as heretical when it appeared in extreme form, this division was, and is, perpetually reinforced by the ceremonial of the Church.

Orthodox rituals, such as churching, baptism and exorcism, which were considered effective against the Devil and his cohorts, were also held to be equally effective against the *xotika*. There are many stories, for example, of how the power of child-stealing female demons was neutralized once the mother was churched or the baby baptized. In other stories, exorcism by a priest would serve to drive away *xotika*, or counteract their power over an affected person. In addition, Christian symbols used to ward off the Devil, such as the sign of the cross, reciting prayers or Scriptures, and sprinkling with holy water, were also effective against the *xotika*. While at the same time, a number of pagan apotropaics, such as black-handled knives, were considered efficacious not only against *xotika*, but against the Devil and his demons as well.

In general, although by no means exclusively, the *xotika* were understood to inhabit the world outside the immediate circle of human daily life, and were generally to be met with in lonely places: "on the mountain" as opposed to "in the city" or "in the village." *Xotika* haunted the intersections of the everyday world and the "beyond", such as caves and the sea-shore. They were encountered most frequently at those times of day when fewest people were normally about; that is, during the midday siesta, particularly during high summer, and in the depths of the night, particularly during the winter. They were most active at those times of the year when important transitions were made, such as the end of the old year and the beginning of a new, or at the turning points of the seasons. Most vulnerable to their attack were those closest to some important change in their life; the most important, of course, being birth, marriage and death.

There was an immense variety of these beings. Some, like Charos, were unique individuals, others were known only as members of a species, while others had an ambiguous status.

Some were visible to all around, and some invisible, although most were able to appear or disappear at will. *Xotika* invisible to ordinary people might be apparent to those said to have a "light shadow", people born on a Saturday.[13] An informant told Lee: "My father would see these beings when he walked at night with my mother; my mother saw nothing."[14] Some people claimed to be able to contact them more or less at will, and some were actually paid to do so.[15]

Everyday thinking is usually vivid and concrete, but liable to be vague, and inconsistent. In consequence, the various types of *xotika* are not clearly distinguished, although they may be vividly imagined. For this reason, the boundaries between the various species are fluid: "what is demon to one may be *Stringlos* to another and *exotika* to a third."[16] So prolific has been the imagination, so isolated the traditions of different locales, and so many the influences upon popular beliefs over the long centuries, that very little that can be said about them is true of all parts of the country. The names given to them vary from place to place. Their taxonomy, has the inconstancy of medieval standards of measurement: "... confusion of the different non-human beings is common . . ."[17] The relationship of one type of *xotiko* to another was probably never very clear in the minds of the peasants.

It cannot be stressed too much that places haunted by *xotika* were not at all rare. They were once to be found everywhere. The Earl of Caernarvon observed of a night journey in the Mani in 1885: "Sometimes the pass was haunted with demons; sometimes unearthly music might be heard along the midnight breeze, or through the sighing of the forest; sometimes the most ludicrous interpretation was placed upon the commonest incident of the day's march."[18] Writing in the mid-twentieth century, G. F. Abbott: "There is hardly a nook or corner of Macedonia so insignificant as not to boast of one or more of these spirits, who make their presence felt and feared in various more or less ingenious ways."[19] Scott McNall could say a village in Attica in the late 1960s: "Almost all the villagers ... have had some encounter with evil spirits, or immediate relatives have told them about such experiences."[20] For this reason it was still considered wise when travelling beyond the confines of the village after darkness fell to carry a black-handled knife. When accosted by a *xotiko* one could create a refuge by drawing a circle on the ground with it, mark a cross in the centre, and stand inside it waiting for dawn to break.[21] Some places seemed to have been centres of such phenomena, such as Mount Pendeli, north-east of Athens.[22]

Clearly, the origin of much of the folklore of the Greeks goes back to remote antiquity, and in some of it can be recognised traces of the familiar myths and legends of ancient Greece. In *The Archaeology of Nostalgia*, Sir John Boardman refers this mythology as "not readily paralleled for its intensity and detail elsewhere in the ancient world." At the same time, he acknowledged the spirited inventiveness of the Greek imagination in constantly reinterpreting the past of the race, and the world around them, and in adapting to the needs and concerns of the present. Thus the ancient stories evolved with the developing life of the people, and in their ever-changing environment.

In order to understand the beliefs and stories about paranormal creatures, it is necessary to ask what purposes those beliefs served in a society that was largely rural and illiterate. From Byzantine times until the last century there have been few cities within the area of the modern state. Athens itself was little more than a market town at the beginning of the nineteenth century. So it was upon the needs and concerns of country folk that these beliefs were focused.

Clearly, they provided entertainment during winter evenings. But certain thematic regularities can also be observed, which have a definite social purpose: for example, that it was dangerous to be out of doors alone, especially in the middle of the day during the summer, and in the middle of the night during the winter, when few people were about. In a society where, for ordinary people, the resources of law and order would have been few, distant and unconcerned, it would be to the benefit of the community to impose a curfew in order to prevent mischief-makers from wandering abroad unseen, and to dissuade potential victims from falling into their hands. Thus the message to potential criminals and victims alike was that to wander abroad alone was to court a terrible fate. Other stories equally clearly gave at least the appearance, and therefore the satisfaction, of explanation of otherwise inexplicable events to those who held a prescientific world-view. Other functions will also become apparent as we review particular themes.

[1] Toynbee 1.
[2] Καμπούρογλου (1920) 77.
[3] Stewart 15.
[4] Lee 126-32.
[5] Bent 7.
[6] Caernarvon 194-6.
[7] McNall 71.
[8] Stewart 108ff.
[9] Lee 126-132.
[10] Caernarvon 111.
[11] Lee 126-132.
[12] Lee 126-132.
[13] Abbott 221.
[14] Lee 126-132.
[15] e.g. in the village of Kalakoli, Karditsas. (Θεοδοσιαδης, 84).
[16] Blum & Blum 95.
[17] Lee 126-132.
[18] Caernarvon 160.
[19] Abbott, 250.
[20] McNall 71.
[21] Stewart 168.
[22] Τσεβά *passim*.
[23] Θεοδοσιαδης (4) 138.

Spirits of Place

Greek folk belief was animistic. It was thought that every cave, every well, every conspicuous tree, every building, was inhabited by a spirit, which might take many forms. Menelaos Tsiklidis has collected a long list of the spirits said to haunt various localities in the immediate vicinity of Vyziki, in Arcadia. They take the form, here of a donkey, there of a black giant, somewhere else of a naked boy, elsewhere of a horse, a priest, a small weeping child, a turkey, etc., etc.[1] Such spirits were thus to be found all over the place. Sometimes the appearance taken by a particular spirit would be bizarre, to say the least; such as the horned priest who beats a cauldron he wears on his head in Lefkochori, near Gortynia.[2]

In general, someone seeing such a spirit should respectfully acknowledge it, but he should not address it, or he would lose his voice. If by any chance he should insult it, it is likely that he would die soon afterwards. When such a spirit howled, someone in the vicinity would soon die.[3]

Of all the common natural features of the Greek countryside, springs seem most likely to have been considered to be inhabited by spirits of various kinds. They might take it upon themselves to appear in many different forms, like that of the spring of Krini at Apeiranthos, Naxos. More usually, they would adopt a single form in which to manifest themselves, such as the spirit which always took the form of a cat, at the spring of Karava, in the same area,[4] or the spirit of the spring of Prasteio, at Kardamylas, Aitolia, which manifested itself as a small white hound.[5]

These local spirits were not always be well-disposed, and many stories carry the warning that a chance encounter with one of them could prove fatal.

An elderly man went on a journey to Voukolia, in Tsakonia, with his mule, when he was ill. When he went to get water, a black giant appeared, kicked him, and told him to "Get out of here!" After that, he weakened, and died within a few weeks.[6]

Springs in caves were particularly liable to be inhabited. There was such a spring in a cave near to the chora of Astypalia named Louki, inhabited by a spirit in the form of a large bird, whose wings could sometimes be heard beating when it bathed. No one drank from this spring without first making the sign of the cross, or else, it was believed, he would die.[7]

On the island of Chios, above the church of Saint Eustratios, next to the wall of the house of Mazanga, is a small spring. Invisible from the road, narrow and shallow, it nevertheless has small caverns and caves inside. At midnight a spirit was said to emerge in the form of a man riding a wild horse, galloping swiftly and noisily along the nearby roads, before returning to the spring. The spirit was called Venia, and it was said that anyone who drank of the spring would go mad. Accordingly, when anyone in the locality behaved in a crazy manner, they would ask: "Has he drunk from the spring of Venia?"[8]

It was once commonly held that if the spirit of the spring at Smiles, in the vicinity of Vyziki, in Arcadia, which took the form of an ox, were to disappear, war would come to the area.[9]

On Gymnovouni in the village of Markasi in Pellinis, Korinthia, is a spring called Goura. Each day at exactly the same time in the afternoon, the flow of water dwindles. Local people used to say that the spirit of the spring came out and placed his foot before the hole from which the water emerges.[10]

In view of these beliefs, it is hardly surprising that offerings would sometimes be left at springs. When James Theodore Bent visited Siphnos, in the mid-nineteenth century, people were still hanging kerchiefs containing honey, milk and eggs in the wells to appease their spirits.[11] In may parts of Greece, new water would be fetched from the local spring or well on New Year's Day, and at the same time offerings such as figs or nuts would be thrown into the water. In Aetolia the spring would be "fed" with corn thrown in by a child who must not speak, either on the way to the spring or on the way back.[12]

River spirits were not always benign. Those at Kefalovryso in Aitolia were described to Lawson as red, grinning devils which sat on the bed of the stream beneath the water. These unpleasant creatures mated with the *lamies* which infested the river banks, and shared and ate the bodies of people they had lured into the water and drowned.[13]

Lakes were also inhabited by their own spirits. Since the 1860s the Lake of Moustos, near Thyrea, in Arcadia, has been believed by many to be inhabited by a great monster which has never been seen, but which has sometimes been heard booming over a great distance. At one period, it made this sound quite regularly, three times a day: in the morning, afternoon and evening. So great was the fear of it that at times people from nearby Astros and Aiannis gathered together and went down to the lake with guns.[14]

The many sink holes (*katavothres*), into which streams and rivers sometimes disappear, only to emerge many miles away, are mysterious places, in the distant past believed to be entrances to the underworld. It is hardly surprising that they were believed to be haunted. The spirits of the *katavothres* would usually take the form of a huge calf, and were generally considered benign, but not universally so.

Benign spirits might become protectors and supporters of an entire community. In the mountainous areas of Central Greece the *koukouvaounes*, or spirits in the form of large white owls with red eyes, could sometimes be heard at night defending their communities. People who looked out, disturbed by the noise, would see small swirling lights in the air all around them.[15]

These "patronal spirits" sometimes fought with each other. When they did this they would appear in forms such as those of rams, oxen, horses, bulls, or dragons. They could be invigorated by drinking milk, and, curiously, they would sometimes triumph over their rivals by using projectiles of lard. On some occasions, such a spirit might seek the help of a man to kill its rival by shooting at it, using his left hand.

The village of Kastania and the neighbourhood of Neohori each had a protecting spirit, both of which lived on Aetos, a peak of Mount Oitis, the one guarding the area to the east of his home and the other to the west. The spirit of Kastania took the form of a cow, and that of Neohori, an ox with golden horns. The two spirits one day fell out over whether a particular piece of land belonged to Kastania or Neohori, and fought over the matter for several days. In the end, the spirit of Neohori forced the spirit of Kastania over a precipice, where it is now buried beneath a mound of stones. The defeated spirit still kicks periodically, which explains the frequent earthquakes in the region. The victorious spirit of Neohori remains lame from the battle, but continues to champion its village, and when anyone beloved in the community is about to die, it announces the event by bellowing.[16]

In the neighbourhood of Arkoudovrisis, in the Western Argolid, village elders spoke of two protecting spirits: one which looked after the area of Krya Vrisis, and one which guarded the region of Tourniki. A local man possessed a herd of forty cattle, and every day he took them out to graze. The spirit of Arkoudovrisis ate his young calves, leaving from forty only one. Its intention was to kill the rival spirit of Neraidovrisis, and by eating the meat of the cattle, and drinking the milk of the one left, he thought he would grow fatter, and so have the substance with which to win the struggle, and so become the only chief of the entire region. One day the man who had lost his cattle chanced upon the spirit of Arkoudovrisis, and said to him: "Tell me, good spirit, why did you destroy forty of my cattle and leave me only one?" The spirit explained: 'I did not eat more because I wish to become the benefactor of this place, if you help me to eliminate the spirit of Neraidovrisis. Listen to what I want you to do. The calf that I left, I left on purpose, to drink its milk. You must slaughter it and cut off its testicles and collect its fat in them. When the spirit of Neraidovrisis turns up, we will both transform ourselves into bulls. He will be black. You will throw the balls with the fat at the black bull, which will be the spirit of Neraidovrisis, and destroy it. When the day came for the contest, and they began to fight, the peasant threw the testicles and the fat over the black bull, and flames darted like lightning. The spirit of Neraidovrisis was destroyed, and from then on the spirit of Arkoudovrisis became lord of the whole region, and a benevolent benefactor of Kali Vrissi.[17]

The nomadic pastoralists, the Sarakatsans, feared the *kalotyches* or spirits of the trees, which are loosed on the world when their trees are cut down. *Kalotyches* means "Good fortunes" and was a deliberately placatory description.[18] They were not alone in their fears. James

Theodore Bent wrote that on Siphnos the woodcutters feared to lie or sleep under some trees; and when they had to cut down a tree that they supposed to be possessed by a spirit, they were exceedingly careful, when it fell, to prostrate themselves humbly and in silence lest the spirit should avenge itself on them as it escaped. Sometimes they put a stone on the trunk of a tree they had felled, so as to prevent the egress of its spirit.[19] A similar custom is recorded in distant Kozani.[20]

Of all tree spirits, those of the plane, poplar and fig-tree were most feared.[21] On Samos, in the village of Lekka, were some plane trees which no one dared cut or prune, or even sleep underneath, despite the shade they provided. It was said that the spirit of these trees had killed one would-be woodcutter, and that whoever slept in their shade would suffer horrific nightmares, and wake up and flee in panic.[22]

It was not merely the species named above, however, which could be dangerous. Trees of more than five hundred years of age were considered haunted in Tsakonia. When someone cut down an ancient oak to feed a kiln he had built, he soon died. This surprised no one. The general feeling was that the spirit of the tree had taken its revenge.[23]

Large and isolated trees near Trikalon, near Corinth, were reputed to be possessed by spirits, and no one dare cut them down.[24]

A rather inconsistent belief in the same area said that dangerous trees are recognisable by the unusual speed and strength of their growth. They *must* be cut down, or their spirits will eventually kill those who planted them. During the mid-nineteenth century, one Petros, son of Papaioanni, planted a walnut tree in the family garden when he was young. It grew surprisingly quickly. When Petros was taken ill, his father immediately cut it down, lest the spirit kill him, and after that, he recovered.[25]

The Earl of Caernarvon wrote that when travelling from Tegea to Megalopolis:

"[W]e observed a knot of oaks so peculiarly fine that we deviated from our path to inspect them more closely. A ruined church was buried under the shade of this gigantic group. Perceiving, or imagining that I perceived, a variety in the foliage of one of these trees, I asked a Greek to pick me a branch. He recoiled from the proposition, and answered: 'Not for the world and all its gold. I should never again have a quiet night, and the heaviest calamities would fall on any person who plucked a leaf from the holy trees; except, indeed, on the feast of the Virgin, when we may safely pick even boughs.'

A peasant standing by confirmed this popular belief, and added that some Mahommedan travellers on this road had picked a bough, and on returning to their homes had mysteriously perished that very evening."[26]

Many tales that initially look like accounts of hauntings are intimately associated with a particular tree, and it is difficult to avoid the conclusion that these are not "hauntings" in the Western sense at all, but that the origin of the story lies in the belief in tree spirits.

Outside Melana, in the field of Dolia, is a spring near a great oak tree, in an area was reputedly haunted by a *foustanella* or kilt-clad apparition. For example, a woman going there to obtain water to take to her aged father saw the apparition sitting beside the spring. She quickly took the water and left. At first, it followed her, but after a while it disappeared without attacking her.[27] Similarly, at Lykoskoufi, at the fig tree of Mastoraki, many people saw the figure of a woman at midday, who would utter inarticulate cries.[28] A fig tree near the village of Samarades, in Arcadia, was believed to be haunted by a spirit which took the form of a lamb. Anyone who came within its shadow, attracted by the bleating, would find that the lamb had suddenly changed into a nereid. He would be held there, lost, for several days; and when he returned, he would be ill or mad, and would soon die; and no medicine or witchcraft would avail to save him.[29] Surprisingly, the spirit of a plane tree in Kartsouni, in Laconia, took the form of a priest.[30]

Due to the inconstancy of popular classification, the spirit of a tree might be given the name of another type of *xotiko*. In Macedonia, the spirits inhabiting trees were frequently referred to as nereids, especially the spirits of the potentially dangerous plane, poplar and fig trees. Labourers in the fields explained their reluctance to rest in the shade of those particular trees, on the grounds that their nereid might resent their intrusion, and inflict a stroke upon the intruder. A special ceremony to atone for such trespass, which involved placing honey and sweet cakes at the foot of the tree, was common practice.[31]

Those who believed that they might have offended the spirit of a tree, perhaps because they had been struck with illness or had been subjected to some misfortune, might sprinkle honey around the base of the trunk, and leave offerings of sweet cakes there.[32] In some parts of the country, when picking fruit from a tree, the country folk would take care not to remove all the fruit, but would leave some on the tree, so that its spirit would not develop a grievance against them, and so that the tree would bear a good harvest on the next year. The same would also apply to harvesting the vines.[33]

Sometimes, it was believed that if a tree was destroyed, the spirit which inhabited it would be "lost," thus identifying the spirit with the life of the tree itself.

A tree was reputed to be haunted at Saravaliou, near Patras by a spirit which appeared either as a light or a dog. Frequently people would see a light above the tree at night, and hear the barking of a dog, although no dog was to be seen. These phenomena ceased abruptly when the tree was struck by lightning, and became a dry husk.[34]

It was once held that each house possessed its own guardian spirit. Its existence might be made known by a thin voice, like that of a little child crying. Occasionally these spirits would reveal themselves in visible forms, such as a dog, cat, or pig. Most frequently, they would take the form of a snake or lizard, although on many of the islands a blindworm or slowworm was looked upon as a house spirit.[35] In some regions, the house spirit was imagined as an unnatural variant of one of those species. In Epirus the house-spirit was pictured as a snake with the head and feet of a cat; on Naxos it was a three or seven-headed snake.[36]

These spirits were usually regarded as benevolent, and, if treated properly, as protectors of the household. Thus a snake appearing in a house in many places, e.g. Kythnos, was treated with the utmost respect; and great care was taken not to frighten it away, for if they did, the inhabitants of the house would die, and the house would be deserted and fall into ruin.[37] In particular, it was believed that it would guard the children of the house.[38] Milk or food would be set out for it. In Zakynthos bread would be left in front of its hole, and when it put in an appearance it would be offered bread and grapes. In Samothrace today "house snakes" are fed milk and in return are expected to keep mice down.[39]

On Karpathos a jug of water would be left out for the house spirit every Saturday night. If the house spirit became thirsty, and there was nothing to drink, it might suffocate the family in their sleep.[40] In general, it was believed that ill-fortune would follow the ill-treatment of these tutelary spirits, such as the collapse of the house, or the death of one or more of its inhabitants. In some places, such as on the slopes of Mount Zirias, in Korinthia, the household spirit was often thought to be a black giant (*Arapi*). Many old houses were thought to have them. They could be heard moving around in the evening, making the floor and stairs creak. People left out water, wine and foodstuffs for them. It was considered that if they were decently fed, they would guard the house and serve the householder.[41]

23

On Zakynthos it was believed that if someone passed by a house as its foundation was being laid, and his or her shadow was caught under the foundations, then the house would be "well-rooted," but the shadow would become a *Pergalio*. It would take the form of a small blue-eyed black child, about four or five years of age. Generally, such spirits were benign and helpful. However, if it were blue-eyed, the inhabitants of the house could suffer from the evil eye. Then they might be liable to a wide variety of accidents. These spirits could, however, cause problems in unexpected ways.

One *pergalio* was present when the lady of a house gave birth to a baby girl, and became particularly fond of her. As she grew up, and became more and more beautiful, he would spend time chatting with her in the evenings, and in time told her of the whereabouts of buried treasure, so that she became rich. Now beautiful *and* rich, her hand was duly sought in marriage by many young men. This made the *pergalio* jealous, and one night he warned her not to marry, or she would regret it. The girl told her grandmother, who in turn told her son. He merely laughed off this women's talk as of no significance. Soon she was married to the son of a rich family. But when her husband first lay down to sleep in the house, the jealous *pergalio* suffocated him. The unfortunate girl entered a convent, and the grieving family abandoned the house, which fell into ruins.[42]

These spirits, sometimes known as "Masters (or mistresses) of the house" were often thought to be the souls of ancestors watching over their descendants.[43] In many places, it was customary on New Year's Eve or New Year's Day to leave offerings for the spirit of houses and of other buildings which were important in the life of the people. Millers on Skyros would throw handfuls of currants figs and walnuts into the mill-stream, and early in the morning, the householders in Chios would scatter fruit, sweets and bread in the various rooms of their dwellings.[44] On Samos, the householder left a jug of water out for the house-spirits every Saturday night as a matter of course. Otherwise they might get thirsty and suffocate the sleepers in their beds.[45]

These generally benevolent house-spirits should be distinguished from the consistently malevolent spirits which occasionally disturbed the peace of a household by making mysterious noises, by throwing bricks and stones, sitting on sleepers' chests in the form of a hideous nightmare or shadow, and by teasing and worrying the inmates of the house at unreasonable hours. These latter were regarded as the disembodied souls of people who had met with a violent death, or whose mortal remains had been buried secretly, without the usual funeral rites. Such persons become ghosts, and roamed restlessly about, visiting their old haunts, inspired with an intense longing for revenge.

It might be assumed that the mere presence of a church building in the neighbourhood would be enough by itself to exorcise such relics of paganism as local spirits or *genii;* but in Greece, the church buildings themselves were often considered to be inhabited by their own spirit. Usually, this was a calf or an ox. These tended to manifest themselves at night, and were sometimes said to be so adorned with precious stones that they would light up the dark interiors of their churches.[46] Many folklorists have drawn up long lists of the spirits which haunted the churches of their various towns and islands, describing them by the forms in which they appeared.[47]

Many church buildings in Athens were believed to be haunted by the ghost of a black cockerel, which would mount the roof of the church and crow three times whenever someone in the parish was to die. The noise it made was said to be perceptibly different from that of ordinary cockerels which were not spirits.[48] The historian of modern Athens, Dimitris Kambouroglou, reported many stories of the haunting of the churches in and around the city by spirits in animal form. In the lower church of the Metamorphosis in the Plaka, on the night before someone in the parish was about to die, a ghostly calf would bellow three times.[49] The small church of All Saints in Ambelokipoi was haunted by a large snake with the head of a cat.[50] People were still occasionally claiming to have seen it at the end of the nineteenth century. In Maroussi, in the northern suburbs of Athens, the old church of the town was still reckoned to be haunted by a calf in Lawson's time. It would also bellow outside the house of anyone in the town about to die.[51]

In the village of Vlachorafti, between Karitainas and Palaiokastro, is a church dedicated to Ayios Dimitrios. Its spirit took the unusual form of a red horse. It was said that it would frequently emerge at midnight from the nave of the church, ride in a protective ring around the neighbourhood, and bring its circuit to an end with a deafening noise back in the nave of the church. Locally it was spoken of with great pride and affection as the "holy horse."[52]

These spirits were usually benevolent. The few that were not were generally forced out of the holy places they had infested, and had to resort to taking up their abode nearby. On a mountain-side near Kalamata is a chapel dedicated to Saint George. The peasants said that during each annual festival on April 23rd, a spirit would emerge from a hole close by and devour one of the worshippers. After some years the people, seeing that there was no remedy for this annual catastrophe, decided to give up the observance of the day altogether. But a week before the next feast, Saint George himself appeared to them all simultaneously in dreams, and assured them that they would suffer no injury at the festival on this year, because he had sealed up the monster. They went to the place from whence it was accustomed to emerge, and found the hole closed by a massive stone, on which was imprinted the mark of a horse's hoof. The people believed that St. George, wishing that the hole should remain closed, had made his horse strike the stone with his hoof. In the mid-nineteenth century, the hoof-mark in the rock was still being shown to visitors. [53]

Sometimes, however, a dangerous spirit succeeded in maintaining its unwanted presence in a church, despite the holiness of the building and all efforts to get rid of it. A quarter of an hour from Agrinion in Trichonias, near the village of Dokimi, is a church dedicated to Saint John, built in a clump of trees. From this church there issued at night a rainbow-coloured spirit with very large eyes, which seems to have possessed the power to attract all those who saw it. Folklorist Nicholas Polites reported a local story to the effect that a countryman who had succeeded in dragging himself away from its magnetic gaze, and thus who was able to tell his tale, nevertheless died shortly afterwards.[54]

These spirits could sometimes act as guardians of the holy places in a very practical sense, punishing those who failed to respect the sanctuary.

There was a shrine in front of the chapel of the Prophet Ilias in the pass of Saita. One day some gypsy women, who were passing by on their way to Pheneos, broke open its door and stole the offerings of money they found inside. A short time afterwards, they saw a large serpent following them along the road. Afraid, they began to run, but when they did so, it merely increased its speed in pursuit. In their panic, they began throwing away the money they had stolen, but it was not until they had "returned" all of it that the serpent disappeared.[55]

Many prominent buildings, and even cities have their protecting spirits. The Patrinella of Patras was a spirit which inhabited the castle of that city and protected it against cholera and plague. When anything bad occurred, she could be heard weeping in the night. It was visible to the naked eye as the body of an ancient statue, built into the battlements of the wall.[56]

The explanation of the appearance adopted by many of these spectres may lie in the once widespread custom of sacrificing an animal, such as a fowl, lamb, goat or calf, on the site of a new building, and of sprinkling the foundations with its blood. This custom has died out only recently in Athens .Rendell Rodd pointed out that the word employed for this proceeding, *stoicheiono*, implies that it is an offering or sacrifice to the *stoicheion* or spirit of the place. The spirit of a church or bridge is thus the spirit of the animal sacrificed at its foundation.[57] Such offerings were also made at the opening of quarries[58] and at the launching of new boats and ships.

The spirits of place, however, did not always manifest themselves in animal form. The church of the Panayia in the district of Alikokkos was haunted by a woman. When someone in the parish was to die, she would sit at the crossroads at midnight and cry out "*Nta patha!*"[59] A story told to Abbott by a native of Chios speaks of a bridge on that island called the Maid's Bridge, popularly believed to be haunted by a Water-Spirit. Early one morning a man was crossing the bridge on his way from the village of Daphnona to Chora, when he met a tall young woman dressed in white. She took him by the hand and made him dance with her. Unfortunately, he was foolish enough to speak to her, and was immediately struck dumb. However, he recovered some days after, thanks to the prayers and exorcisms of a priest.[60] Many of the churches of the island of Skyros were thought to be haunted by little shepherd girls.[61] These beliefs in local spirits which appear in human form may have a very surprising and sinister origin.

Popular tradition contains evidence that important foundation ceremonies may at one time have included human sacrifice. Reference to this practice may occur in the very well-known poem about the building of the bridge of Arta. The central pile of this bridge fell down every time it was built, until the master-builder dreamed that it would only stand firm if his own wife were to be buried alive in the masonry. He therefore summoned the good woman, instructing her to dress as for a special occasion, and then found an excuse to persuade her to descend into the central pile, whereupon the workmen heaped earth in over her. Thus the bridge stands fast to this day.[62]

A similar problem was encountered in building the equally famous bridge of Karitainas over the river Alpheios. A witch told the Frankish lord of the castle that the only way to secure its successful completion would be by the sacrifice of the lady of the castle. She sportingly consented, and was walled up in the centre of the bridge, with only a small hole left for her to breathe. She lasted for three days, but her cries were said to have been audible for an entire year afterwards.[63] A parallel tradition is found in relation to other haunted bridges, such as that of Mavrozoumainas, near Meligala, in the Peloponnese.[64]

The haunting of a spring in Kastanitsa, in Tsakonia, is explained in a similar way. A sharp increase in the flow of water from out of the ground once threatened the village. Local people tried to block the outlet and divert the flow, but without success. So they took an old woman, wrapped her in cloth, and lowered her on a rope into the hole. Then they let go of the rope. She fell, and her body jammed and blocked the flow, so that the increase was diverted to another outlet. Afterwards she became a spirit and haunted the spring.[65]

Rendell Rodd reports a belief still prevalent in his day that some unscrupulous people would attempt to lure the unwary to the site where the foundations of a building was being laid, and without their noticing, to lay the foundation stone across the shadow which they cast, or over a thread surreptitiously attached to their persons. It was thought that those whose shadows had been "buried" in the foundations of a building in this way would die within the year. For this reason, children were warned by their parents to keep away from building sites, lest their shadows be "stolen." A writer contemporary with Rodd quoted a monk of Zakynthos as saying that only fear of the law kept the people of that island from actually burying human beings under works of especial importance: a Jew or a Muslim being especially marked out by tradition as a suitable victim.[66]

Lawson called the practice of burying a person's shadow as "a compromise between actual murder and total disregard for the traditional rite."As an alternative to trapping someone's shadow in the foundations, some piece of a person's clothing, hair or nail parings would be buried there. Since the person thus selected was expected to sicken and die within the year, an older person was usually chosen "out of philanthropy."[67]

In consequence of this practice, as late as the middle of the twentieth century, sickness was still sometimes attributed to the belief that the soul of the invalid had, unbeknownst to them, been "imprisoned" in some manner in the foundations of a construction.

Charles Stewart records the story of an islander on Naxos of a sickness attributed to the construction of a well in the village of Apeiranthos. Every day, when the well was being dug out by her sons, their mother would bring them lunch at their workplace. Then one day she fell ill. Her jaws simply locked and she could not open her mouth to speak or eat. After a couple of weeks, when she had taken no solid food, they took her to hospital in Athens. There she was fed intravenously for about six months, until she was able to open her mouth a little and take some solid food. After some time, they brought her back to the island, but she immediately withdrew to her bed, and spent most of the next two years rejecting all company. Then one night, when everyone was asleep, she went outside and threw herself down the well. Next day, someone heard her cries and called her family, who managed to pull her out, and put her to bed. She had recovered her voice and the full use of her jaw. She explained that she had jumped into the well because she had seen two bearded men in a dream who instructed her to do so. She herself thought that her shadow had been trapped in the well at the time of its construction, and by diving into the well, she had reunited herself with her shadow.

This explanation recalled for Stewart the traditional account of the construction of the main church in Apeiranthos, which had required the shadow of the master builder's wife. The workers building it would labour during the day, but each night their work would be reduced to rubble. Then the master-builder dreamed that he would have to erect the structure over his wife's shadow. The next day he told her to stand in such a position as to cast her shadow over the foundation stone. Ill-advisedly, she did as he wished. The building stood fast that night, and from that point onwards there was no problem, and the people of Apeirinthos had their church. Three days later, however, the builder's wife died.[68]

It seems clear that at a comparatively late date, a substitute human sacrifice was considered preferable to that of a mere animal. This practice may have been in part designed to provide a spirit for the building, on the understanding that if it was left untenanted, some malign spirit from "outside" might take up its abode there, with disastrous consequences for those who would later use it or live in it. The "killing", whether real or symbolic, may have been to provide an "acceptable" spirit-tenant who would become a benign guardian.

Greece is a land of mountains and islands, in which communication between one place and another has always been difficult. This has always favoured the independent growth and development of local traditions, and accounts for the immense fertility and variety of Greek folklore. Although not strictly spirits of place, many locations have their own unique traditions of some species of *xotika* which exclusively haunted their own neighbourhood. It is perhaps in these purely local traditions that the peculiar richness of Greek folklore is most apparent.

The people of Arachova believed in species of spirits which were helpful to them in their daily labour. The *Perganta* were always present where the women were working, either indoors, in front of their houses, or in the fields. They would help them when they combed the wool or spun cotton, because they particularly loved these occupations, so that people would say of an industrious woman, "She works day and night, like a *Perganta*." Similarly, in the same area, the *Gorgonia* were beautiful boys who haunted the vineyards and the arable fields. They would be seen digging, ploughing, hoeing, watering, and performing all the work of the land. They would especially help those who did their work well, who might themselves be described as working "like a *gorgoni*."[69]

Peculiar hauntings of particular spots are innumerable, and a few examples must suffice. Many in Karytaina claim to have seen a red-skinned woman, known as Koutsocheria, combing her hair.[70] An evil spirit known as Koulocheris, which appears half way between a vampire and a satyr is said to haunt the neighbourhood of Monastiraki, Drama.[71]

In the "Haunted Hole" (Stoicheiotrypa) on Mount Gkiona, near the village of Sykia, in central Greece, a century or so ago, people used to see small old men with beards which reached down to their waists and large eyebrows which reached the crowns of their heads, who were reputed to be very wise.[72]

In the countryside around Sparta there is a woman dressed in white who suddenly appears on the roads in front of male travellers and beckons to them with a golden hand. In the neighbourhood of Tripolitsa there is a similar phantom, which behaves in exactly the same way, but she beckons with a black hand.[73]

The villagers of the Midland Plain of Attica feared the appearance of a strange gaudily feathered bird of ill-omen called the Gynaika-Pouli. Its bizarre appearance presaged catastrophe. It was seen flying near Spata, where the International Airport is now situated, just before the Asia Minor catastrophe of 1922; and it was seen above the vineyards of nearby Koropi just before the outbreak of the Second World War.[74]

Some hauntings peculiar to specific localities were bizarre, to say the least. In Arcadia, nymphs would appear under the bridges over the rivers during the night as weasels.[75] One part of the island of Anghistri was haunted by diaphonous, jelly-like humanoids with webbed fingers who emerged out of the sea, and another part by a giant hen and its brood of giant chickens.[76] The villagers of Philoti feared a large nightbird with the face and ears of a man which haunted Mount Dias. It was the spirit of a man cursed by God to wander far from the habitations of men for ever for slapping Christ in the face before his crucifixion.[77]

[1] Τσικλίδης (2) 2:140-2.

[2] Τσικλίδης, (2) 2:144.

[3] e.g. Κωστάκης 78.

[4] Πολίτη, 1:192.

[5] Πολίτης 2:192.

[6] Κωστάκης 77.

[7] Πολίτης 1:191.

[8] Πολίτης 1:192.

[9] Τσικλίδης (2) 2:140.

[10] Πολίτης 1:193.

[11] Bent 13.

[12] Megas 45-6.

[13] Lawson 276.

[14] Τσικλίδης (2) 2:280-1.

[15] Γιαννουλάκης (1) 299.

[16] Γιαννουλάκης (1) 298-9.

[17] Τσικλίδες (2) 1:227.

[18] Fermor (2) 39.

[19] Bent 13.

[20] Αυλίδου 142.

[21] Abbott 244.

[22] Θεοδοσιάδης 80.

[23] Κωστάκης 77.

[24] Σταματούλη 699-671.

[25] Πολίτης 1:178.

[26] Caernarvon 112-3.

[27] Κωστάκης 74.

[28] Κωστάκης 74.

[29] Πολίτης 1:215.

[30] Πολίτης 1:216.

[31] Abbott, 244-5.

[32] Abbott 245.

[33] Παπακωνσταντίνου 348.

[34] Πολίτης 1. 215.

[35] e.g. Rodd 170; Περδικα 145.

[36] Πολίτης 2:244.

[37] Πολίτης 2:244.

[38] Bent 211.

[39] Στάμκος 33.

[40] Νουάρου 237.

[41] Τσικλίδης (2) 1:80-1.

[42] Πολίτης 1:187-8.

[43] Abbott 258.

[44] Megas 43-4.

[45] Πολίτης 1:184.

[46] Lawson 261.

[47] ' e.g. for Skyros, Περδικά 2:131.

[48] Καμπούρογλου 507, 512-3.

[49] Καμπούρογλου 485, 507, 511, 513-4.

[50] Καμπούρογλου 507.

[51] Πολίτης 1:211; Lawson 261-2.

[52] Τσικλίδης (2) 2:204.

[53] Lawson 261.

[54] Πολίτης 1:196.

[55] Καρασούτας 454.

[56] Πολίτης 1:197.

[57] Rodd 168ff.

[58] Καμπούρογλου 3:148.

[59] Bent 132.

[60] Abbott, 246.

[61] Περδικά 131.

[62] Μολίνος 75-9.

[63] Τσικλίδης (2) 2:200-2.

[64] Θεοδοσιάδης (1) 362.

[65] Κωστάκης 76.

[66] Rodd 168-9.

[67] Lawson 264.

[68] Stewart, 406-7.

[69] Πολίτης 1:188-90.

[70] Θεοδοσιάδης 82.

[71] Αυλίδος 126.

[72] Γιαννοπούλος (1) 301.

[73] Θρακιώτης (1) 368.

[74] Τσικλίδης (1) 1:80-1.

[75] Τσικλίδης (2) 2:202.

[76] Τσικλίδης (1) 1.190-1.

[77] Κεφαλλινιάδης.

The Beautiful People

Belief in the nereids was perhaps the most widespread and common of all the beliefs of the Greeks in *exotica*. Even today, many living people in many parts of the country will, under appropriate circumstances, admit to having heard or seen them.

At the beginning of the twentieth century, John Cuthbert Lawson wrote: "As for the peasants, let them deny or avow their belief, there is probably no nook or hamlet in all Greece where the womenfolk at least do not scrupulously take precautions against the thefts and the malice of the Nereids, while many a man may still be found ready to recount in all good faith stories of their beauty and passion and caprice. Nor is it a matter of faith only; more than once I have been in villages where certain Nereids were known by sight to several persons (so at least they averred); and there was a wonderful agreement among the witnesses in the description of their appearance and dress. I myself once had a Nereid pointed out to me by my guide, and there certainly was the semblance of a female figure draped in white and tall beyond human stature flitting in the dusk between the gnarled and twisted boles of an old olive-yard.

What the apparition was, I had no leisure to investigate; for my guide with many signs of the cross and muttered invocations of the Virgin urged my mule to perilous haste along the rough mountain-path."[1]

The nereids are beautiful creatures in human form, usually, but not invariably, female. The females are always dressed in white, decked with crowns and garlands of flowers, and often wear a veil, which flutters behind them in the wind. Frequently they are said to have exotic legs: one being that of a goat, donkey or cow. Or their may both be human but reversed, with the toes pointing towards the rear.[2]

Generally speaking, they were looked upon as light-hearted, irrational, capricious beings, of more than human grace and beauty. To be compared to a nereid was the greatest of compliments; to be said to have a nereid's eyes or a nereid's hair was the highest praise that could be bestowed on a woman's beauty.[3] Their powers included the power of riding through the air, and of passing from one place to another with the swiftness of the wind, of becoming suddenly invisible, and of slipping through chinks and small holes. They were also known to be accomplished in all womanly arts, to spin and weave, and sing as no mortal woman could. For a housewife, to be said to sing, to dance, to cook, to weave, or to sweep like a Nereid, was the ultimate accolade. They were not immortal, but their lives exceeded those of men tenfold, and their beauty did not fade until death.

Although there was a feeling of awe, not unmixed with fear, in the popular attitude towards them, they were not usually considered hostile towards those who did not cross them in any way. However, their nature was by no means always benign.

There are literally hundreds of place-names in Greece with the word *nereid* incorporated into them. They especially haunted streams, springs, caves and bare hill and mountain tops, for example, on the beach outside the "Nereid Cave" on Mount Yerousi, in Adiata, on Syros. There is a "Nereid Hill" midway between Thessaloniki and Kilkis, on the summit of which the nereids of the river were said to dance in the light of the moon. They washed their white dresses in the creek of Rousounara on Mykonos. If you disturbed them, they would disappear in whirlwinds. If these touched you as they passed, they caused blisters, which could only be cured with holy oil.[4]

Theodore Bent found belied in nereids on the island of Keos to be particularly all-pervasive.

"When [the mists] cleared away we had a glorious day, and we simply revelled in the lovely scenery of Keos after, bare, ugly

34

Thermia. The road winds along very high ground; on either side are deep, dark valleys leading down towards the sea, with fantastic rocks and full of oak trees; in the dim morning these great oaks, with their huge stems and stretching arms, looked weird enough. No wonder the superstitious Keotes people them and their cliffs with Nereids; somehow in Keos these mystic beings seem to be brought into closer union with humanity than elsewhere. "They often," says the housewife, "steal her clothes, her sheets, and bed linen, but they nearly always return them." Very often the Nereids have children by human men, for the most part malicious, evil-disposed children. "Charon must have been your sponsor and a Nereid your dam," is a frequent expression of abuse to naughty children. For those who are supposed to have been struck by the Nereids when sleeping under a tree the following cure is much in vogue. A white cloth is spread on the spot, and on it is put a plate with bread, honey, and other sweets, a bottle of good wine, a knife, a fork, an empty glass, unburnt candle, and a censer. These things must be brought by an old woman, who utters mystic words and then goes away, that the Nereids may eat, undisturbed, and that in their good humour they may allow the sufferer to regain his health."[5]

The nereids showed a mild preference for places difficult for men to reach. Near the village of Yeleni, on the slopes of Mount Ziria, in Korinthia, is a saddle of land high on the northern slopes, quite inaccessible to man and beast, covered with two belts of undergrowth, which is always dark green throughout the driest summer. It is known locally as the "Nereid Garden", for there, it is believed, the nereids make merry.[6] Many mountain tops were also thought to be the abode of nereids, such as Mount Hymmettos outside Athens,[7] and the highest peak of Zakynthos.[8] Despite this taste for wild places, they could approach human dwellings, and sometimes could be heard, or even seen, from the houses of the villagers.

The anthropologists Richard and Eva Blum and Blum were told: "I remember sitting at the window once in 1938. It was about midnight I heard the nereids and *aerika* passing by with drums and violins. They were dancing, and going towards their square where they always went to dance, a square which is up towards the mountains. These nereids do not harm anyone, but when you heard them you became frightened and you shivered."[9]

The places particularly haunted by the nereids were sometimes thought to have uncanny qualities. The wooded valley of Gavros, near Kollines, in Arcadia, was one such. A group of exiled Kollianates returned from Australia once went on a trip there. Their watches stopped, they lost all sense of time, panicked, tried to find their way back, got lost, wound up in some completely different place, and could not understand how they had got there. Parents will not allow their children near this place.[10]

Encounters with nereids seem to have been nothing less than frequent.

Traveller Dorothy Ratcliffe was told in the 1930s of a man who lived on Mount Parnes, who said he had "... once met a nereid at noonday, when all his neighbours were indoors resting from the summer sun. He saw her trying to get a thorn out of her foot. She was standing in the shade of a fig tree, leaning against the trunk, and she was dressed in sunlight. He called to her and she ran away. He ran after her and caught her as she stooped below the boughs of a pine, which hit him on the head. He said that kissing her was sweeter than eating honey." The traveller's informant added that after meeting her, the man was not seen for a long time, and when he did get back home he was trembling, and had lost his wits.[11]

Researchers Richard and Eva Blum were told the following: "I've met the nereids. When I was a soldier I was walking home and I stopped near a river to eat some bread and drink some water. When I tried to drink, the nereid started throwing pebbles in the water to try to frighten me. I saw the point and gave up trying to drink there." Another witness said: "I myself have seen the nereids. I was working for the great landowner at the time, and late one night, about eleven pm., I was leaving his house. I had a bucket of water on my head. As I went past the pond in front of his house some creatures started throwing stones at me. I turned around and saw a very beautiful girl all dressed in white sitting at the pond. She had a mandolin and was playing a most touching melody. Someone else ... about the same period saw a whole group of these people, the nereids, going towards the beach. They started from that pond and were all playing instruments of one sort of another and dancing."[12]

Despite their general lack of malice, danger, was never far away. A man at Nigrita was returning from the fields one night when he saw under a tree by the roadside a young woman adorned with gold pieces, like the holiday dress of the peasant girl in those days. She was very beautiful, and, he said, looked like a bride. No sooner did he speak to her than "his tongue was tied" and he became dumb, and remained so for the rest of his life. This was a common result of addressing nereids.[13]

It was widely believed that Nereids could be brought under human control by those who succeeded in snatching some item of their clothing or a personal belonging, and keeping it closely hidden. It was generally the nereid's veil, or kerchief, which was seized, and she who had lost it had to forego her power of invisibility, and follow her master as his wife and slave. However, the nereid bride would soon tire of human companionship, and would long for the freedom of the mountains. Thus she would be for ever searching for the stolen item of clothing which bound her to her human master, and if she found it, or persuaded her husband to restore it to her, she would promptly leave him, even though, if she had in the meantime become a mother, she could never be readmitted to the dance of her sisters. This belief seems almost universal, although in the island of Cephalonia, it was held that an escaped nereid would have to return to her husband after seven years in the rather unlikely event that during all that time he never once left his house.

The story of nereid-human marriages is found all over Greece. The villagers of Exochora near the peak of Livas, on Zakynthos, were said to have intermarried *en masse* with nereids and to have inexplicably disappeared.[14] More usually, however the descendants survived, and some families were said to have nereid blood in their veins, evidenced by their good looks. The famous Mavromichalis clan, which dominated the peninsula of the Mani in southern Greece for centuries, was said to owe its hereditary good-looks to the marriage of George Mavromichalis with a rare sea nereid.[15] The good-looks of the Brettos family of Acharnes (or Menidi) in Attica received the same explanation.[16] Lawson was introduced to a Thessalian peasant who believed that he had a nereid grandmother; and he was certainly credited with it in his village.[17]

Sometimes the nereid never really adapted to human society or accepted the marriage. A youth of the village of Sgourokephali who had great skill upon the lyre, used to accompany the Nereids to their cave and play to them. One of them especially excited his admiration, and he resorted to a wise old woman of his village to seek to learn how he might gain her for his bride. The old woman bade him seize her by the hair as cockcrow approached, and never let go, whatever forms she might assume in order to terrify him, until the cock had crowed. Accordingly, the next time the nereids took him to their cave, he played for them, as was his custom, but when the hour of cock-crow drew near, he flung his lyre aside, seized hold of the nereid he loved, and clutched her by the hair. At once she changed her under his hand into a dog, then a snake, a camel, and at last into the appearance of fire. When the cock crew, the other nereids disappeared, and he was left with his prisoner, who now reassumed her real form. She followed him quietly to the village. Within the space of a year she bore him a son. But during all this time she never uttered a single word. He returned to the wise woman to help him break this silence. She instructed him to heat the oven which then stood outside every Greek cottage, and then taking their boy, to say to his nereid wife, "As you will not speak to me, I mean to burn our child," and to feign the action of doing so. Once more he took her advice. The nereid found her voice, but only to cry, "You dog, release my child!" She tore the infant from his hands and fled. The story goes on to say that, being a mother, she could not return to her sisters, but took up her abode in a nearby spring, where every now and then she might be seen holding the child in her arms.[18]

The Corinthians told a much more sinister tale of a nereid marriage. A workman used to like to get up very early each day to go to work. One day he got up earlier than usual, before daybreak. On the road he heard the sound of voices. Going nearer he saw nereids swimming in some water. They had discarded their petticoats and left them on the grass. Quickly he darted towards them and snatched one up. When the nereids saw him they stopped singing, came out of the water, snatched up their petticoats, and vanished. Only one was left behind, she whose petticoat the workman held. He took her home and she became his wife. In time she bore him three children. She was a good wife in every respect except one. Whatever he bought her in the way of clothes, she constantly pleaded to have her original petticoat returned to her. Then one day he thoughtlessly gave in to her importuning and said that she could have it. She waited one day, until he was away working in the fields, then she put it on. Then she murdered her three children, went outside, locked up the house, and vanished. When her husband returned he called and knocked, but received no answer. Then he remembered that a nereid would be compelled to stay as long as you kept an item of her clothing. He realised what a fool he had been to give her the petticoat, and that he had lost his wife. But at least, he consoled himself, he still had their three small beautiful children. When he got inside the house, it was to find them lying dead on the floor.[19]

Sometimes the roles were reversed, and it was the Nereid herself who fell in love with the mortal, and those who were thus chosen were sure of all good fortune and success as long as they remained faithful; but should the mortal partner stray from strict fidelity to his wife, the Nereid's vengeance would be unremitting, and he might pay with his life.

Richard and Eva Blum were told the following tale, which an informant's father used to relate: In the past when some handsome youths were accustomed to sleep under the shadows of some trees, the nereids would come and tease them, and wanted to marry them. One of them mentioned what was happening to his grandfather. He said that a girl came to him every noon while he relaxed under a tree, a girl who was very lovely and, very different from all the others he had ever met. His grandfather understood immediately that she was a nereid and suggested to the youth that he get hold of her scarf. He said that he was afraid to touch her but his grandfather assured him that there was no danger; and that if he really wanted to marry that girl, getting her scarf was the only way he could hope to keep her. The youth did snatch her scarf, after which she meekly followed him, and their marriage soon followed. Years went by and they had a child, the nereid proving herself an excellent wife and mother. Then one day at the annual village festival there was dancing in the square. The nereid was by far the best dancer. She was, as everyone said, something out "of this world." When she danced, her feet seemed not to touch the earth. People commented on this to her husband, and he was very proud of her. At one point, when she was taking a rest, he told her how beautifully she danced. She said that she could do even better if she had her scarf, and asked if he would return it to her - just for a single dance. He decided that there was no danger of her disappearing any more, since they had a child, and so he handed over the scarf. This time, her dancing was truly superb. As it was coming to an end she turned to her husband and said, "Watch me take the dance into the sky." Then, after a turn, off she went, dancing into the sky, never to return.[20]

In a few stories, male nereids appear, particularly those from Crete. The well-known Cretan chieftain, Captain Christodoulaki, of Sphakia had disappeared for a long time as a child, and was sought for all over the mountains. It was only after a long search that his brother, who was calling his name, heard his voice answered, and going to the spot, found him in a strangely dazed condition. At length, he realised that he had been carried off by a man and a woman to the high point where he was found; he could hear the voices of the seekers calling, but was prevented from answering by the woman, for they were nereids. At last, the man and the woman fell out, and he took the opportunity of their coming to blows to answer the cry, and when his brother drew near, they disappeared.[21]

From Crete also comes another story, taken down by the traveller Robert Pashley in the early part of the twentieth century, as he heard it from the lips of a Sphakiote. "Two men, his informant told him, went one fine moonlight night into the mountains to hunt the Cretan wild goat, They heard a great tumult, and at first supposed it to be a company of people coming to fetch snow to take to the city; but as they drew nearer, they heard the sound of musical instruments. Soon they discovered these were not mortals, but an assemblage of goblin beings, all clothed in varied garments. Both men and women, on foot and on horseback, a multitude of people. All the men were white as doves, and the women as beautiful as the sunbeams. They were carrying something which resembled a bier, and as they passed along they sang: "We go, we go to fetch the lady bride, from the steep rock, a solitary nymph." The mountaineers determined to shoot at them. As the shot was fired, those who were last in the procession exclaimed, "They've murdered our bridegroom. They've murdered our bridegroom!" and shrieked and fled."[22]

A Macedonian story told of a shepherd who one moonlit summer night tended his flock in a meadow. Suddenly he was startled by the sound of many musical instruments, such as drums and pipes, in the distance. The sounds drew nearer and nearer, and at last there appeared before him a long chain of maids dressed in long white robes and dancing to the tune. The leader of the dance was a youth carrying in one hand the wooden ,vine-flagon used by the peasants. He halted in front of the shepherd and held the flagon out to him. The shepherd accepted the offer, but before proceeding to raise the flagon to his lips, he, according to the custom of the country, made the sign of the cross. At this, both dancers and leader vanished, the music ceased, and the shepherd was left alone, holding in his hand in lieu of the flagon a human skull. His piety had saved him from any consequences more serious than a serious fright.[23]

On Zakynthos and Samos people believed that the nereids disappeared into springs, behind which were doorways leading into their world.[24] In Gortynia, sounds of musical instruments could sometimes be heard coming from the Nereidovouna of Mezenikou.[25]

The nereids gave birth like humans, and desperately desired male children. On Kimolos, on a hill overlooking the town are some caves inhabited by nereids near some windmills. One night the midwife was sent for by a nereid of the cave, saying, "If the child turns out to be a boy, you will be happy. If it is a girl, we shall tear you into four parts and hang each one in the cave." When the baby arrived, it was a girl. Determined not to be quartered, the midwife lied and said that it was a boy, immediately swaddled it tightly, and went home. After eight days had passed, when the time came to remove the swaddling clothes, the nereids discovered the truth and were horribly disappointed. One of their number went to the midwife's house and knocked on her door. The midwife was expecting this. She also knew that if you answer the first knock of a nereid, you become mad, so she ignored it and survived their wrath.[26]

Nereids were supposed to steal newly-born human children, and sometimes to substitute their own. Therefore, the house-door was kept shut for many days after a child was born; and Greek mothers never left their babies to the care of older brothers and sisters, but took them out when they went to the fields, fixing them in little leather hammocks to a tree, or to three sticks crossed in a shady place, where they could be continually kept in view. In many places, mothers dressed their baby boys as girls because the nereids' preference for boys was so well-known.[27]

Those nereids which danced near the chapel of Faneromenis, on Milos, were said to be particularly fond of stealing children and substituting changelings. If a mother suspected that a nereid child had been substituted for her own, she would leave it all night lying naked on the altar in the chapel. If it was found dead on the next morning, then it had not been a human child. If it lived, then it was.[28]

Dorothy Lee was told by a man whose mother-in-law had just given birth to a child that the nereids had tried to take it during the night. They were in the act of carrying her out, but had not yet got her outside the house when his father-in-law woke up, and raised his rifle to fire. At that moment, the cock crowed, and they dropped the baby and fled.[29]

The name nympholepsy was given to those afflicted with depression or fits of frenzy. A preference for solitude was also ascribed to their pernicious influence. Those who were struck by nympholepsy were said to avoid their own kind, to spend their time wandering abroad along lonely paths, and returning late at night. Death would overtake them at a young age. People born on a Saturday were especially susceptible to their spell.[30] A girl from Halandri, outside Athens, the daughter of a priest, took to wandering the slopes of Mount Pendeli on her own in this manner. When she disappeared from home altogether, she was said to have run away to join the nereids, and people subsequently claimed to have seen her dancing on the slopes of the mountain.[31]

On Serifos, Bent found that ugliness in babies was also attributed to the baleful influence of the nymphs. "No sooner had we spoken of nereids than demarch's daughter, a woman of fifty or more, at on developed a desire to talk and tell her story as to what had happened to her as she was staying in Constantinople with a cousin of hers who had just had a lovely child which had become ugly owing to the influence of the nereids; so the mother was determined to take child and lay it on a marble monument in St. George's Church. Having done this, she laid it on a grave for, a while and took Miss Kousoupis with her without telling her anything about it. The child was left for five minutes on the grave, and then the mother gave it to Miss Kousoupis to carry; and as they went away, owing to the mother having given Miss Kousoupi no notice of what she was doing, she looked round, and the child died in a fortnight, and she herself suffered from headaches giddiness, and general wasting, and was brought back to Seriphos in a dying state. So her mother took her to the monastery of the archangel, where we had just been and there they lived for forty days until she recovered; but even now she said she was liable to fits of faintness and giddiness." Bent adds: "The vividness of the narration and the excitement of the narrator quite convinced me that she believed that what she was telling me was true." On Samos, impotence was put down to seduction by a nereid.[32]

Nereids were said to grow particularly harmful at noon, and children were warned not to stray out of sight at that time, for the nereids were known to strike their victim dumb, especially if he replied to their enticing questions when they addressed him with fair words. The islanders of Melos used to believe that nereids danced in a dried up river bed outside Chora near the church of the Virgin of the Apparition (*Panayia tis Faneromenis*). In appearance they were beautiful women, except that their legs were donkeys' legs. It was believed that anyone who chanced to see them would die, and that neither doctors nor medicines would avail to save them. If a child became paralysed, the parents would test whether the problem was that the child had stumbled upon the nereids or if the condition was curable, using a rather drastic procedure mentioned above, which seems to have been traditional on that island. They would take the paralysed child to the Church of the Apparition (*Faneromenis*), strip it, and lay it upon the marble altar slab, leaving it there throughout the night. If, when they returned, the child had died, they would say that the nereids had taken it, and that its doom had already been irrevocably sealed. If it was still alive, they would say that the problem had some other cause, and then they would take it to a doctor.[33] This practice was declared illegal during the nineteenth century.

Nereids frequently acted as temptresses. Scott G. McNall was told by a shepherd in Attica at the end of the nineteen sixties: "One night when Yorgos was out with his sheep, he fell asleep. He said: 'I woke up and there were two women who looked very much like two women from the village except that they had on gold and white gowns. The older woman asked me if I wanted to sleep with her daughter. I knew then that they were evil. I stirred up the fire, and they disappeared in a whirlwind.'"[34]

Both at night and in the middle of the day, it was their practice to kidnap young men. They would hold them for several days, seducing and exhausting them, after which the nereids would later give birth. In the meantime they fed their captives with their own strange firm black bread and other foods. When the young men were returned at the boundary of the mountain, they would be exhausted, pale and thin. If they were not exorcised within a short period of time, they would sicken and die.

There is on the summit of Mount Hymettus a small round space known as the "level," which was carefully avoided at the hour of noon by any shepherds who might be pasturing their flocks on the mountain. They told the story of one of their number who had, in ignorance, ventured within this charmed circle, and who was at once overpowered by a whirling wind which knocked him prostrate, and kept him a prisoner there until late in the afternoon.[35]

Young men in love with them would be liable to seizures and strokes. People could sometimes be quite clinical about the phenomena which the nereids were used to explain. Richard and Eva Blum were told simply: "they cause symptoms which are the same as brain haemorrhage."[36]

Researchers have been told personal stories suggesting that encounter with the nereids could have tragic consequences.

The Blums heard the following story: "My husband has had some experience with the effects of the nereids...one night he ... heard the neighbour's horse annoying ours so he'd gotten up to see. Well when he was up he didn't see the horses but decided to go out and urinate. It took him a very long time. I thought something must have happened to him so I went out to see. I saw him standing, staring towards that old spring that was near by. He stared and stared and then suddenly fell down, just as if he were dead. I carried him in and put him to bed, and for some time he was sick. He didn't remember a thing when he opened his eyes, but I'm sure he was staring at something, and that something was the nereids.

Something still remains of this shock, for when he sees blood or someone in pain, he faints."[37]

Charles Stewart was told this story by the dead man's widow: One day a man was approached by his wife, while working in his hut, to make up a load of wood for her. She was not his wife, but a nereid who appeared in the form of like his wife. Her husband told her that first they would have sex, and afterwards he would see to the wood; and this is what happened. On the next day, when the man got home, his wife asked if he had brought a load of wood. He protested, that he had given her a load on the previous day. When his wife denied it, he reminded her what had happened. His wife was outraged. That night his genitals began to swell up and cause him pain. This went on for several days, so they called in the priest to read an exorcism over him, and also medical doctors, but no one was able to help him, and he died."[38]

The consequences of falling into the hands of the nereids could be much more immediate. An English traveller heard among the Mainotes of Taygetus that: "Three maids of exquisite beauty, but with the legs and the feet of a goat, are to be found dancing around the summit of Scardamyla. No man may approach them with impunity. Should any one unwittingly venture within the precinct, he is first fondled and embraced and made much of; but, then thrown headlong from the precipice, and dashed to pieces on the rocks below."[39]

The whirlwind, which is not uncommon in Greece, even in summer, was a manifestation of their presence. It was caused by their dancing, and with this wind they might lift the wayfarer off his feet and bear him away through the air. Therefore, as late as the nineteenth century, even in Athens those who saw the dead leaves and dust circling, and felt the whirlwind near, would bow their heads and whisper: "Milk and honey be in your path."

The Athenians told a story about a girl named Klino, who one day shortly after Independence mysteriously disappeared after last being reported by eyewitnesses to be passing just outside the Tower of the Winds in the Roman Agora. Her parents, thinking that someone had kidnapped her, searched everywhere for her, but could find no clues at all as to her whereabouts. She was discovered one week later lying unconscious on the ground where she had last been seen, outside the monument, her clothes torn to rags. When she was taken to the doctors she was found to be half mad, and raved about being kidnapped by the nereids, who had danced around her, then carried her away in a whirlwind. Her parents took her to the church to be exorcised for eight consecutive days, and at last, her sanity seemed to return. She said that the nereids had snatched her away and taken her to the top of a mountain to be one of their company. But she had wept every day, and after some time they lost their patience with her, slapped her face, and returned her to the spot from whence they had originally taken her.[40]

The nereids presided over and controlled a ceremony known as the "Kleidona," or the "Speechless water", which took place on St. John's Day (Midsummer Day). The previous evening a new earthen jar was filled with water, by a boy if possible, that all the conditions might be complete. Whoever filled it must not speak while doing so, and if spoken to must not answer. Then a company of girls who had associated themselves together to test their fortune, would drop into the water, each for herself, some token which would be easily recognizable - a button, a ring, a key, and so on. The jar was next covered with a cloth, securely fastened, and left out all night, so that the Nereids might place it under a spell. In the morning all the girls would meet, and the jar would be opened by the same individual who closed it. The girls would then each in turn sing a rhyme, while the person holding the jar put in his hand and brought out the first object touched. The line of the rhyme which accompanied the action was held to apply to the girl to whom the object pulled out at that time belonged.[41]

The power of the nereids could sometimes be destroyed by humans. In the spring of Gravari, near the tortoise cave, in past ages a nereid would come up from the plain of Katsanas, and bathe in the pool at midday. For fear of her, local people dare not sleep on the plain or approach the pool near this time of day. The landowners wished to sell their land near the spring, but were unable to do so, because no one dared cultivate it for fear of the nereid. Then a strong young man from Lykouria, Ilias Spiliotis, offered to kill the spirit if the landowners would give him ten *stremmata* of land near the spring in return. They readily agreed. He cut an oak staff and went to wait at the spring before midday. When she arrived, he dashed at her, raining blows upon her back and shoulders. Taken entirely by surprise, the nereid gave out a strange cry and dissolved in smoke. She was never seen again.[42]

They could also be used as a source of skills. A skilful Cretan lyre player was always thought to have acquired his craft from the nereids. Someone who wished to do this would go to a crossroads in the middle of the night, draw a circle around himself in the ground with a black-handled knife, and settle down inside it to play the lyre as best he could. Soon the nereids would arrive. They would seek to lure him outside the circle by any means they could, and for his own safety, he had to resist them. He would ask their help to play the lyre and they would make many promises, seeking to get him to put his hand outside the charmed circle. He had to resist these blandishments. If he placed just so much as the tip of his little finger outside the circle, they would straightaway cut it off. But if he played from within the circle until cockcrow, they would dance, and in doing so, would give him the power to play the lyre skilfully before they vanished.[43]

In a cave on Mount Bourino in Kozani is a cave in which water drips from the roof. This water is said to be from the breasts of the nereids and will cure illnesses. Whoever wishes to take some of the water to a sick friend or relative must observe certain precautions. He must travel to the cave without speaking to anyone, bringing green lamp to light it inside, and a green pot. When he had filled the pot with water, he had to leave some part of his clothing behind, and return home without speaking to anyone. In particular, as he exited the cave, he must not be perturbed by anything he heard, nor must he turn back to see what was going on behind him. If he did, the water would lose its power, and he would lose his mind.[44]

The modern nereids are clearly the direct descendents of the ancient nymphs. These were of various kinds, classified according to their characteristic haunts. In ancient times the nereids proper were nymphs of the sea, but the term "nereid" came to be the general term for all the ancient nymphs. In modern times, the ancient word for "nymph" has come to mean "bride", and all nymphs are now indiscriminately referred to as *nereids*.

The ancient nymphs were divided into subspecies based on the geographical region over which they presided. Nereids presided over the seas, Naiads over springs and rivers, Dryads or Hamadryads over trees and forests, Oreads over mountains, Limoniads over meadows, Limniads over lakes, marshes and swamps. Some nymphs were named from their precise locality: like the Acheloids, or nymphs of the River Achelous, and the Kiffisid nymphs of the Kifissos River.

They were usually thought of as beautiful girls who could sometimes be observed singing and dancing. They were always female and beautiful. Neither divine nor human. They lived so long as to be practically ageless, and always appeared at about the age at which women would get married. Although most were gentle and amorous, others were associated with the wilder aspects of nature and were akin to female satyrs. The nymphs took on stereotypically female roles such as weaving. In mythology they brought up children, and were thought sometimes to save and rear children who had been exposed.

Although not divinities, they were the objects of cults and could answer prayers. They were often worshipped with Pan. Altars were dedicated to their worship in a nymphaeum, a monumental fountain or well. Here, they were regularly honoured with garlands, and on special occasions with sacrifices. Such a place is the Cave of the Nymphs in Kefalari of Kifissia.[45]

It is probable that the actual spots in recent centuries thought to be haunted by Nereids were once dedicated to the worship of a nymph, or nymphs, in ancient times. Rendell Rodd claimed that in a certain village in the highlands of Arcadia, in the neighbourhood of which was a spring and a grotto which bore evidences of the worship of the nymph to whom tradition maintained that it had been sacred. The expression was still in use among the men when they wish to describe the beauty of one of the village maids: "She look like the nymph under the tree."[46] Bent records: We … saw … an interesting cave with the inscription over it, "the temple of the nymphs", cut in the rock. Here we have an old centre of nymph worship, and here we still find wonderful stories of Nereids and *genii loci* associated with the spot. Travellers who cross a certain stream close to here, more especially at midnight or midday, are exposed to the danger of being possessed; and to cure such cases it is customary to prepare and place at a spot where three roads meet, or hang in the wells, some bread wrapped up in a clean napkin, and some honey, milk, and eggs, to appease the nymphs."[47]

At the grotto of the Seven Virgins outside Kalymnos the story is that seven virgins retired into the cave to escape the attentions of some pirates, and were never heard of again. However, the slips of petticoat attached to the bushes outside show that, like the nymphs, they would enable women who prayed for a child to conceive. Cotton and woollen threads are still attached to nereid-haunted springs.[48] Clearly this moral tale was an attempt by the Church to "baptise" the cult of the nymphs in that place.

Many tales speak of a queen of the nereids. In Eastern Greece she was the "Queen of the Mountains." In Zakynthos she was the "Great lady"; in Thrace the "Great Lady" or the "Good Lady."[49] She was even the unofficial, uncanonised and churchless Saint Kalo to the ordinary uneducated Athenians of the eighteenth century.[50] In folk tales she may appear as "the Mistress of the Earth and Sea" and "the Beautiful One of the Earth."[51]

The area of Krinofyta at Ayios Athanasios near Kleitorolefkasias, Kalavryta, is nereid-haunted. A particularly handsome shepherd boy who went there to graze his sheep at midday was admired by the nereids. He was swept away forthwith in a whirlwind to Mount Lykoureiko, where the queen of the nereids had her palace. She kept him captive with her for many days. One day, when he observed that she had wandered some distance from the palace, he slipped away and made his way back home, and told of all that had happened to him. Not many days after, however, the nereids seized him again, and this time, he did not get away, for he was never seen again.[52]

Normally, however, the Queen of the Nereids was fiercely virginal, and treated any men who chanced upon her with great severity. She was larger and fiercer than her companions, and a dweller in the mountains and forests. She danced and bathed with her companions in pools and streams. In Kardamyli, Aitolia, they said that it was dangerous for an unmarried youth to venture out in the middle of the night from Phonia. He would meet the nereids, led by their very beautiful leader, she would strike him with her golden belt. After that, even if he returned to his village, he would be an idiot, and doomed constantly to roam the mountains, ever seeking the nereids.[53] Oddly enough, in Aetolia the Queen of the Nereids was considered to have the culture of tobacco under her special care.[54]

Saint Artemidos was especially prayed to for nymph-struck children. He is a Christian incarnation of the goddess Artemis, the ancient queen of the nymphs. On Keos St. Artemidos was known as the patron of weak children who had been struck by the nereids, and a church dedicated to him, some little way from the town on the hill slopes, used to be the appropriate place to seek a cure. Theodore Bent recorded: "thither a mother will take a child afflicted by any mysterious wasting, 'struck by the Nereids,' as they say. She then strips off its clothes and puts on new ones, blessed by the priest, leaving the old ones as a perquisite to the Church; and then if perchance the child grows strong she will thank St. Artemidos for the blessing he has vouchsafed, unconscious that by so doing she is perpetuating the archaic worship of Artemis . . ."[55] On Milos such children were laid on the altar of the church of the Virgin or at the entrance to certain catacombs, in a similar rite.[56]

The stories about nereids, and belief in their existence, were perhaps more widespread than those about any *xotika*, raising the question as to what purpose they served in traditional Greek society. It has been suggested that they reflected male anxieties about women.[57] However, this fails to take account of the fact that women were the usual bearers and transmitters of such stories and beliefs, so there must be a presumption that they served the needs primarily of women. It is clear that the "message" of most of the stories about nereids is that men who find themselves in lonely places, and are confronted with beautiful girls or women, must on no account have anything to do with them, or they will inevitably suffer for it. Thus it is a defence of the institution of marriage by the mothers and grandmothers who transmitted these stories on behalf of their sons' and grandsons' future wives, and also a measure of protection for their daughters and granddaughters. In addition, however, since many of the young men forcibly abducted by the nereids were assaulted to the point of exhaustion and madness, a point rarely stressed but usually at least hinted at, there is a clear element of prurience in many of the stories. The stories about changelings have the effect of relieving parents of responsibility for ugly or otherwise unacceptable children, while those about nympholepsy seem to be pseudo-explanations of various morbid mental or social conditions, such as clinical depression.

[1] Lawson 131.
[2] Stewart 181.
[3] Rodd 173-4.
[4] Πολίτης 1. 291.
[5] Bent 220-1.
[6] Τσικλίδης.
[7] Πολίτης 1:295-5.
[8] Θεοδοσιάδης 80.
[9] Blum & Blum 114.
[10] Τσικλίδης 2.87.
[11] Ratcliffe 152-3.
[12] Blum & Blum 118.
[13] Abbott 242-3.
[14] Θεοδοσιάδης 80.
[15] Fermor (1) 50.
[16] Πολίτης 1. 334.
[17] Lawson 134.

[18] Rodd 178-9.
[19] Πολίτης 1:345-6.
[20] Blum & Blum 112.
[21] Rodd 179-80.
[22] Pashley 2:217-8
[23] Abbott 246.
[24] Θεοδοσιάδης 82.
[25] Θεοδοσιάδης (4) 137.
[26] Bent 23.
[27] Θεοδοσιάδης (4) 76.
[28] Πολίτης 1:323.
[29] Lee.
[30] Πολίτης 1:325.
[31] See full story in Tomkinson (2)
[32] Ποιλίτης 1:389.
[33] Ποιλίτης 1:323.
[34] McNall 70.
[35] Πολίτης 1:295-5.
[36] Blum & Blum, 114.
[37] Blum & Blum 118.
[38] Stewart 4.
[39] Quoted in Rodd 175.
[40] Tomkinson (1) 90.
[41] Megas 136-8.
[42] Καρασούτας 449.
[43] Πολίτες 1. 413.
[44] Θεοδοσιάδης (4) 137.
[45] Tomkinson (2) 54-5.
[46] Rodd 174-5.
[47] Bent, 13.
[48] Abbott 243.
[49] Θρακιώτης, 297-8.
[50] Fermor (1) 183.
[51] Fermor (1) 180-181.
[52] Καρασούτας 441.
[53] Θεοδοσιάδης (4) 81.
[54] Fermor (1) 181.
[55] Bent 221.
[56] Bent 36.
[57] Blum & Blum 218.

Elemental Forces

Many of the *xotika* of Greek tradition have parallels in the folklore of other nations, in particular, the giants and ogres. These creatures, with their enormous strength and limited intelligence seem designed to personify some of the brute forces encountered in nature. Of these, the most prominent in Greek folklore is the ambiguous figure of the *drakos*.

It was believed on Andros that the history of that island could be divided into several "ages": the age of the *drakoi*, the Hellenes, the Venetians, and finally the Turks. When men first arrived on Andros there was still a very old *drakos* living there.[1]

The *drakoi* were used to explain the existence of the old towers which are to be found dotted about the countryside. One story goes: There were once two *drakoi* who were brothers: one decided to build the tower of Markotantoulou and the other the tower of Saint Peter's. Each tower was two hour's journey from the other, and a mountain lay in between, yet each wanted to build his tower taller than the other. When they had finished, the brother who built the tower of Markotantoulou travelled to see his rival's work. He was astonished at how much his brother's tower was taller than his own. When his brother took him to the top to show him the view, he was overcome with jealousy. He pushed his brother down; but as he was falling, his victim clung onto him, and they both fell to their deaths. The marks made by their talons, as they tried to grasp the building as they fell, can still be seen in the masonry.[2]

Situated on the mountain slopes of southern Evia are a series of mysterious megalithic structures the origins of which are unknown, called "Dragonhouses". The first western sighting was by John Hawkins in 1797. Since that time some twenty-five have been located, but they have all suffered, to differing degrees, from the attentions if visitors. All are intricately built from large boulders, stones and slates. The remains suggest that some may once have had an upper floor. Local lore attributes them to fearsome *drakoi*.

Various hypotheses have been put forward to account for the existence of these mysterious buildings. They have been attributed to semi-barbaric tribes, transhumance shepherds, such as the Sarakatsans, and quarry workers. They have been seen as temples, forts, guardhouses, and cattle byres. Their position is not of any strategic importance, which seems to rule out their use as forts. Remains found inside show them to be ancient. The oldest is an inscription on a shell in the ancient Chalkidic script, suggesting a range of dates between the sixth and fourth centuries BC.[3]

The following story is told about the dragon house near Profitis Ilias. The *drakos* who lived there had a paramour who lived near the village of Rouklia. He would visit her each might on his horse, which would wait for him until dawn. The woman did not love him, but she could not get rid of him. One night, she asked him if he feared anything. He replied that the only thing he was afraid of was her brother's dog. She thought about this for some time, trying to work out how she could use this knowledge to rid herself of his attentions. She noticed that it was the *drako*'s custom each evening to leave his horse with as much barley as would be necessary to keep it content throughout the night, so that when it had finished, it would understand that it was time to go. One evening, the woman mixed sand with the horse's barley. When dawn broke, the horse was still eating its fodder, and the *drako* still with the woman, when her brother arrived with his dog. He chased the *drako* up the mountainside. There was a secret passage which led to the mountain peak, and the dragon's lair. But a little before the *drako* reached the hole which was its entrance, the dog arrived. The *drako* fell down on his knees in terror, and today, in the rock, a paw mark of the dog and the outline of the knee of the *drako* are still visible. Then the *drako* shouted for help to his sister in Roumeli.

She soon arrived, but found that her brother had already expired. She buried him in entrance to the passage, and raised two large stones over it, which are still there today.[4]

It is clear from the story above, that the Greek *drako* is not the familiar dragon of western lore. In the Anglo-Saxon literature dragons were scaly creatures which could fly whilst emitting fiery and noxious breath, and having a poisonous bite. Their normal occupation was to guard burial mounds, and the hoards of treasure buried within them. Usually, *drakoi* in Greek folklore are not fire-breathing flying reptiles. They are large creatures of fearsome powers and, usually, of human or near-human shape, similar to the northern troll or ogre. The *drakos*, when thought of as a giant, sometimes has a spouse quite as big, strong, and stupid as himself. The family is occasionally increased by a number of daughters who are remarkable for their size, strength and taste for human flesh, and who inherit their parents' lack of wit.

In a cave near Platanisto, on Evia, a *drakos* lived with its wife and daughter. When the locals first acquired muskets, they employed them to rid themselves of him.[5]

One characteristic story goes that there was once a king who had an only daughter. She was a lovely, beautiful maiden, and her name was Photeine. Two princes in the neighbourhood were enamoured of her. They both were marvellously tall and strong giants of men, and were known as *drakoi*. Not surprisingly, the king feared them greatly. One day they both came to Photeine's father and asked for his daughter's hand. The king, on hearing the object of their visit, was seized with alarm and did not know what to do, for he feared that, by preferring one of them, he would incur the wrath of the other. So he devised a plan. He proposed to his daughter's suitors to throw the quoit, saying that the one who beat the other should become Photeine's husband. They readily agreed. Each took up a rock of an equal size and flung it with all his might from the same spot. But neither of them won; for the rocks both fell in the same place. Photeine's father then bade each of them build each a castle of the same size, saying that the one who finished first, should take his daughter. They began and ended their task at exactly the same time. As this had failed to solve the problem, they decided to settle the matter in single combat, but they fought with such great a fury that they both fell dead. When the Princess Photeine heard that these brave suitors had fallen victims to their love for her, she grieved profoundly and resolved to live and die a maiden. She retired to a lonely part of her father's dominions, and there spent the remainder of her life in saintly seclusion.[6]

Sometimes a *drako* can be identified with a historical personage. The ruined fortress of Phyle, on Mount Parnes above Athens, was said to have been once inhabited by a *drako*. On one occasion he summoned all the other *drakoi* of the mountains to attack and capture the city of Athens. At that time it was surrounded by a wall, so the leader of the *drakoi* had a large drum constructed which could be sounded by the wind. They left the drum on the mountain when they attacked the city so that the Athenians thought that the *drakoi* were still far away, and made no preparations to meet an attack or close the gates. In this story, Kambouroglou saw a distant folk memory of the occupation of the fort by Thrasybulos in 404-3 BC in opposition to the Athenian oligarchs, and his attack and seizure of Piraeus to liberate the city.[7]

On Zakynthos it was believed that the giants were tall and powerful beings with one single eye which blazed like a fire. The first giants were created by the devil. They lived in the bowels of the earth and raised up great rocks and built towers and other large buildings. When they were born, they were immediately held in a river, and from that time they were not vulnerable to gunshot or iron except in that part of the body their mothers held them.[8]

The "single eye" inevitably calls to mind the *cyclopes* of Homer's *Odyssey,* and these Zakynthian giants may indeed be their last descendents. The single eye blazing with fire, together with the habit of hurling rocks, as narrated in the *Odyssey*, suggests that the cyclopes were originally the personification of volcanoes.

Another type of ogre very frequently encountered, especially on mountain summits and in grottoes, springs and wells, was the "Moor" or "black giant," (*Arapis*). These large black men were usually imagined smoking a long pipe.[9] Those they were displeased with they tormented, and they were even said to kill when seriously offended. In Crete they were known as "Saracens", and were used to frighten children.

A black giant who carried a beam on his shoulders kept a treasure in one of the springs of Trikalon, Corinth. It was not a good place to pass at night, and people avoided it. Then one night, a certain Panos, full of brave spirits on his way home from a wedding, decided to drink from it. He found the giant barring his way, and pulling out his gun, fired at him with his left hand. Unfortunately, the giant caught him a blow with the beam he bore, and when Panos got home, he took to his bed and died a few hours later.[10]

A moor known as Deliklimpapas lived in a small cave in Nauplio below the Palmidi Fortress. He would occasionally issue out at night and kill people at random. He held a small pipe in his hand, but when he approached a man, he would grow in size, and his pipe with him, so that when he puffed out smoke it would cover the sky.[11] On the small islet of Lanado opposite Syra, a black giant threw stones at vessels passing by at around midnight.[12]

Sometimes the "black giants" were spirits of place. This raises the interesting question of how Greeks came to see such apparently alien figures as part of the paranormal "fauna" of their own land. They might have been introduced into Greece by the Turks from the literature of the Arab world, where the black giant who is a genie is a familiar figure. Rendell Rodd suggests an origin for the figure of the black giant in the *Arabian Nights*.[13] But so separate were the lives of the Christian Greeks and their Turkish masters that it seems unlikely that there should have been such a transfer from the literature of the dominant minority community into the oral tradition of a subordinate and generally hostile majority. Lawson considered two possibilities. The first is that wealthy Ottoman homes may have employed black slaves, and these may have come to be credited with magical powers; although it is difficult to see how they could have been transmuted into *xotika*. Or they may have been sacrificial victims. For this alternative, Lawson marshals some impressive evidence. The "black giants" seem to be frequently associated with wells, the sinking of which would have no less required a sacrifice as the erection of a building. Rodd reported that in Zakynthos a distinct preference for offering up Muslims existed, and they may have been considered generally dark-skinned. There is a legend of the immuring of a black man in the bridge of an aqueduct near Livadeia, in Boiotia.[14]

Lamies usually appear in folk belief as female ogres: hideously deformed monstrous and malignant females with infantile minds, hungry for human flesh, particularly that of babies. They are also frequently represented as withholding the water from a district, until a human victim has been offered. They could be described as female *drakoi*.

Athenian folk belief tells a story of a *lamia* who hid inside a well and lived on the blood of living beasts. At length she was shot by an aggrieved peasant whose two only oxen had been devoured by her. No one had ventured to attempt to shoot her before, for fear that any bullets fired at her would return and strike their owner. But this wily peasant took the precaution of shooting at her with his left hand. The body of the *lamia* was three fathoms long, and it was said that where her blood had poured out over the ground, no green thing would ever grow afterwards.[15] The island of Anaphi was particularly troubled by *lamies*.[16] Many springs in the neighbourhood of Nymphasias, in Arcadia, were inhabited by *lamies* who thirsted for human blood.[17]

Sometimes the *lamia* was a beautiful woman. The *lamies* of Megara, which haunted crossroads at midday and in the evenings seem hardly distinguishable from *nereids*.[18] Generally, beautiful women who are *lamies* rather than *nereids* were characterised as such by the crude violence they displayed towards the people who encountered them.

The *lamia* in the ravine of Manolia, near the River Lefkas, above the road to Kalavryta, appeared as a woman who sat and combed her long fair hair at the spring of Mustapha Effendi in the middle of the day and in the middle of the night. If anyone approached the spring at those times, she would beat him, and he would either die or become very ill.[19]

The *lamia* of Kokkini, in Dervenochoria, was a tall, slender, beautiful young woman who lived in a spring at Kokkini, just above the village of Stephani. She did not bother or disturb anyone who did not bother her, except that people would frequently hear the sounds of crockery, cutlery and saucepans as she washed them in the spring. One day, however, a shepherd returned from Kokkini bruised and bloody. His explanation was that the *lamia* had attacked him. The *lamia* was said to take animals from the shepherds and eat them raw and drink their blood. Author Menelaos Tsiklidis was told by his father that his own grandfather's grandfather killed her. He was hunting for hare one evening when he suddenly came upon the creature. She said: "Don't kill me; I won't bother you." But he was frightened, and he shot her." She cried out a curse and disappeared. About a month later, her killer developed a strange herpes-like condition about his mouth. It spread across his face, and his flesh peeled off until he died. Another version, however, attributes the death of this *lamia* to a man named Kyriazis. The *lamia* had also cursed him, and he died of cancer within a few years.[20]

Another story told at Stephani was that a shepherd married a *lamia*. This unusual match did not work out. She ate his flock one by one until he had no animals left. Then she ate the other members of his family. At last, realising his own danger, he escaped; presumably just in time.[21]

In old times, it was said, there lived a *lamia* in a spring at Doumbri, outside Arachova. Whenever the townspeople held a festival, they had to provide the *lamia* with someone to eat, so that she would leave everyone alone and not spoil the festivities. Each time, before the beginning of the feast, they would cast lots to find who it was who was to be offered to appease her. Then on one occasion, the lot fell upon a very handsome youth, the son of the leading citizen. His parents pleaded with him to slip out of the town to avoid his fate. He refused, saying that he would deliver the town from the problem once and for all. They youth's parents tried with entreaties and tears to make their son change his mind, but his will was steadfast. He went to the spring of Doumbri to face the *lamia*. She saw him approach, and seized him, but as she did so, he transfixed her with his spear and killed her. Then he returned to the town with the good news that in future, the festivals could be held without anyone being sacrificed, and the townspeople were able to live in peace.[22]

The origins of the *lamia* lie in classical literature where she was a fair maiden, so fair that Zeus himself succumbed to her charms. The result of this admiration was a number of beautiful children, which, however, Hera, the jealous spouse of the "Father of gods and men", snatched from their mother's arms. Their mother went to hide her grief and despair among the rocks of the sea, and there that her beauty decayed, and she became a cruel, hideous monster, the terror of children. Another ancient tradition describes her a beautiful sorceress who upon occasion assumed the form of a snake. According to another legend, Hera, furious that her husband had cheated on her yet again, punished the unfortunate Lamia by compelling her to eat her own children. She want mad, and developed a taste for children. Other stories said that despite the murder of her first children, Lamia had more that were called *Lamiae*. These were blood-sucking half-human and half-serpent creatures with four feet. The front feet had claws, and the back two were cloven hooves.

Sometimes, a *drakos* would take the form of a serpent, sometimes a fearful serpent with a human head.

There is a cave in Kefalonia, near the ruins of ancient Kranis, which was dug out of the rock by a *drakos* to use as its home. The marks of its claws can still be seen on the rock, scratched above the entrance.[23]

Snakes can under certain circumstances grow to a great size in Greece. When they do, they cause fear and alarm, and quickly take on a preternatural character. There are many stories of "hauntings" by such serpents in the area of Achladokampos, in the Argolid.[24]

At the Karakalos Monastery on Mount Athos, a huge serpent came out of the sea and took up residence in the monastery. It did not bother anyone, and the monks left it alone, regarding it as their "house snake", although one of unusual size. It was supposed to be fatter than the embrace of a man, and many metres long.[25]

An old chief shepherd (*tselingas*) known as Nicholas the Black was going to Kastri with others to purchase animals, when darkness fell, and they looked for somewhere to spend the night. While they were sleeping, a huge serpent approached the old man and began to swallow him. His companions heard his cries, but by the time they had fully awoken only his legs were visible. Without losing any time, they attacked the monster with their knives, ripping the snake open and plucking out old Nicholas, almost dead. They revived him by rubbing him all over, but he could remember nothing of what had happened to him. When morning came they resumed their journey to Kastri. One year later the same company were going to Kastri on business again, and they came to the place where they had killed the serpent. They approached the spot where the snake's bones were lying, and said "Look, these are the bones of the serpent which nearly swallowed you last year. We killed it and got you out." The old man did not believe them, and said "What! This thing swallowed me?" With his foot, he gave a kick to the serpent's bones. As he did so, a pointed bone pierced his big toe. His foot soon swelled up, his health deteriorated, and within a week, he was dead.[26]

Below Lykalono, is a place where a large snake which lived in a cave used to lie in wait for goats or sheep. It would wrap itself around them and break their bones, smear them with saliva, and then swallow them whole. It was said to have been killed by lightning. Around the turn of the last century, an elderly couple were passing along the road going to collect salt. It was afternoon and the sky was generally clear, except for a small cloud over their heads. An electric storm broke out. They looked up, and saw coming down a gully towards them a huge snake. It crossed the road in front of them, and going down, slid around an ancient willow tree. The lightning struck it, splitting the tree and killing the serpent.[27]

During the 1860s there were persistent reports, reported in the local press, of large serpents roaming the central plain of Arcadia in the marshy area near Lake Kandilas, frightening hunters. Some claimed that they had horns, and roared, and, perhaps not surprisingly, thoroughly frightened the hunting dogs. They were reported to emerge from narrow gorges and sink holes.[28] The skeleton of huge snake was said to have been found in the area of the Red Rocks of Kolosourti, in the gully.[29]

The foundation legend of the great monastery of Megaspilion, as related to Lord Caernarvon by his guide, involved a huge man-eating serpent. A little girl was tending a flock of goats, when she observed one of her animals with traces of water on its mouth coming from a thicket where she knew there was no spring, Anxious to discover the source of the water, she followed the animal until it reached a secluded spot, where the Virgin Mary appeared to her in the shape of an old woman. She commanded her to summon a priest, and enjoined him to set fire to a neighbouring wood, which was then tenanted by a huge serpent that habitually devoured passers-by. The priest arrived, a torch was applied to the thicket, and the serpent surrounded by a sea of flames. Its dying agonies were terrible to behold, and its groans horrible to hear. At length it became still in death, and the country was delivered from the scourge. Yet even now sometimes a low, strange, hissing sound falls on the traveller's ear at midnight, freezing his blood, and filling him with terror. A spring was found where the serpent died, and over it, a shrine was erected to the Virgin. The girl was sunsequently treated as a saint, and the shrine became in time the mighty monastery of Megaspelion.[30]

One curious belief was in the existence of the *liokorno*, a large serpent with a single horn, which was believed to be a panacea for illnesses. In the Mani, they said that this horn was especially effective in the cure of poisonous snake bites.

One day a priest of Kefallonia was walking on a road by a beach when he saw an innumerable swarm of snakes approaching the sea, following such a single-horned creature. He carefully observed their progress, while prudently keeping well out of the way, and saw the *liokorno* approach the sea, pause, rub its head on the sand, and then slip into the water. When the snakes had all disappeared, he went down to the place where the *liokorno* had paused, and searched for the horn. When he found it, he took it home.[31]

There waere also persistent stories of enormous serpents with heads resembling that of an ox. It is said that in 1835 the port of Fonia, below Mount Roufia, in Ileias, was flooded by water running off the mountain, and several such creatures were spotted. Locals quickly took the word to Pyrgos, and people came out from the town to look for them, but by then, they had all disappeared.[32] In May 1891 the deputy Nomarch of Thessaly and a forester from Keramidas were hunting in the forest of Rapsani, near Tyrnavos, when they heard loud noise of breaking twigs near the chapel of Ayias Triadas. They prepared to aim their rifles, as they expected deer or other wild game to appear. But what they saw was a huge serpent with the head like an ox and two small horns. It must have been about two and half metres long. They both shot at it, missed, and then took to their heels.[33]

The *laphiate* of Naxos was a two headed serpent. There were also three and seven-headed serpents. The *topakades* of Thrace resembled the traditional dragons of northern climes. Huge winged serpents, they guarded the treasure which lies beneath ancient ruins. Once a year, usually on the eve of SS Constantine and Helena, they would spread out their treasure and clean it, to prevent it from deteriorating, before burying it once more.[34] Sometimes, the *topakades* decide to offer their treasure to a man in his sleep in return for a sacrifice, perhaps of a human life. If the dreamer agreed to the deal, he was informed of the whereabouts of the treasure, and allowed to draw from it. If, however, he mentioned his good fortune to a third person, he would get nothing.[35] The *drako* which guarded the cemetery of Nymphasia, in Arcadia, was a serpent with a large head and wings.[36] The steep creeks and caves of Karpathos were haunted by a monstrous bird-headed serpent.[37]

It is hardly surprising that belief in buried treasure is a prominent element in Greek folk beliefs, even though hoards in ancient graves were rare. During the Byzantine period, the popular imagination thought that the purpose of erection of ancient monuments was either as a magical prophylactic, to ward off evil, or to guard buried treasure. Some English travellers during the Turkish period thought the same, especially the English "milordi." It is hardly surprising, then, that many Greeks became inclined to think that all archaeologists were treasure hunters. The Turks, however, thought that they were descendants of Greeks who had fled the land prior to the Turkish invasion, had inherited traditions as to the location of their family treasure, hurriedly buried before their ancestors had fled, and had returned to recover it surreptitiously.[38]

One very widespread and very bizarre belief about buried treasure was that at night the gold coins came to the surface of the ground and grazed, like snails. The coins would bump against the rocks and stones and could be heard clinking. In some places, it was held that treasure was attracted by human faeces. This superstition was used by one hopeful local to explain to researchers Richard and Eva Blum why there were piles of human faeces stacked up in his neighbourhood.[39]

At Kalyvia, in two places, Riza tou Pyrgou and Hasnas, this phenomenon of clinking coins could be heard at night. In both places there are ruins of buildings dating from the Turkish period. At Hasnas was a storeplace, while at the other taxes were paid.[40] The same phenomenon was also said to occur near some ruins above Ano Liossia, outside Athens.[41]

Hidden treasure was usually guarded by a spirit, which frequently took the form of a black giant, dragon or serpent. It was frequently believed that anyone who discovered a hoard of treasure would be unable to remove it safely without some sort of blood sacrifice to appease the spirit that guarded it. For example, on Karpathos it would be necessary to cut ones finger,[42] or on Samos to cut one's hand, or else it would turn to carbon.[43] In the castle of Monovyzas, in Arcadia, it was believed there was a treasure of gold coins which grazed during the night guarded by a *drako*. At this time it was available to anyone prepared to shed blood for it.[44] This belief was connected with the widespread idea that to search successfully for hidden treasure it was necessary to use a lamp which burned human fat.[45]

A Cretan tradition seems to record a transition from human to animal sacrifice in this matter. A shepherd saw one day in a pool a fearful black giant, who, with one hand reached to touch the peak of the mountain, and with the other, the bottom of the pool to scoop up water, and held in his hand a golden florin. The shepherd ran to tell the villagers, and an old man in the village told him that there was a great treasure in that place, sealed with a magic spell. Whoever dug there would find a stone slab, with the treasure beneath it. Three youths immediately ran to the place. They had dug down and found the stone slab, but they were themselves found dead beside it. After that, no one dared try his luck with this treasure. Then some time afterwards, a Jew went there, and read on the slab that in order to raise it safely it would be necessary to slaughter twenty-one siblings on top of it. The country people were at first appalled when he told them, but being rather resourceful, they found a hen with twenty one chickens, and butchered them on the stone. Then they lifted up the slab, and found the treasure.[46]

On Tinos there was a tradition that someone once killed his child to secure the hoard of coin he had discovered.[47]

Frequently, the spirit which possessed a treasure would communicate its whereabouts to a mortal in a dream. This was not always to the man's advantage. It is a common belief that if someone dreams of treasure and tells others about it before going to find it himself, he will only find something worthless, usually carbon, when he gets there.[48]

Such a story explains the building of the bridge of Alibei in a tradition of Trichonia. One night a villager dreamed of a treasure of golden florins filling a bull's skin in a place which was afterwards known by that name. He thought no more of it. He received exactly the same dream a second night, and thought it curious, but of no significance. When he dreamed of it on a third successive night, he became convinced that there must be something in it. So he went to the place he had seen in his dream, dug, and found a bull's hide full of gold coins. He removed the treasure, little by little to his house, where he hid it. Unfortunately, an evil-minded neighbour saw him, and reported his good luck to Alibei, the Turkish pasha in Vrachorio. Without passing any judgement, he arrived, seized the coin and hanged the unfortunate villager. In time, the matter came to the ears of the Sultan. He decided to issue a *firman* authorising the seizure of the gold and the beheading of Alibei. This was not out of sympathy for the unfortunate peasant, nor because of outrage at the gross violation of justice, but simply to get his own hands on the gold. Hearing what was afoot from friends at court, Alibei immediately hired workmen and began to build the bridge which now bears his name. When the officials arrived from Constantinople, he was able to tell them that he had not reported the gold because he was employing it to improve the countryside, and showed them the building work as proof. Thus the bridge was built, and Alibei escaped the cupidity of the Sultan.[49]

The belief that one can be told about hidden treasure in a dream is an ancient one. An attic life of Sophocles has Herakles appear to Sophocles in a dream and tell him where a golden crown was hidden on the Acropolis. He in turn informed the city authorities, and when they had located it, they used the money from the sale to erect a temple to Herakles in the city.

In north of Lykouria, high on the mountainside of Fakia, is a deep and dark cave. In its depths lived a black giant and a nereid. In the very far depths was hidden a great treasure, which the black giant guarded. He watched over the treasure during the day, and the nereid took over at night. At night, the gold pieces which made up the treasure turned into sheep and grazed the hillside around the cave. If anyone chanced to approach them, the nereid would take away their power of speech. One night, she left the sheep unguarded, and went to Epachto, where there was a meeting of all the nereids of the region. By ill-chance a band of robbers came upon the sheep, and tried to seize as many as they could. However, as soon as they seized upon one, and tried to hold it, it would disappear. They soon realised that the sheep were phantoms and fled in terror, and the sheep became florins once more. When he learned what had happened, the black giant reprimanded the nereid; and from that point onwards, he guarded the treasure himself, day and night.[50]

Treasure was not always stored underground. In the eighteenth century it was believed by many that a treasure in gold coins lay at the top of one of the columns of the ruined temple of Olympian Zeus, in Athens. It was said to be guarded by a black giant who lived in a brick hut on the top of one of the columns, and that he could sometimes be seen after dark leaping from column to column.[51]

Snakes were often guardians of treasure. Above Kamara, on Andros, is an ancient megalithic monument consisting of two upright stones and a third laid horizontally across the top of them. According to a story from Palaiopolis, at the foot of one of the uprights is buried a great treasure, and under the other lives a fearful serpent. No one dare dig for the treasure for fear of choosing the wrong stone.[52]

In the area to the southwest of Arachnaion, in the Argolid, named Pigadaki, where there are sheepfolds, there is said to be a buried treasure guarded by a dwarf. People say that anyone who tries to recover the treasure will meet the dwarf, who seems particularly vigilant and aggressive, and who is likely to take pre-emptive action against treasure seekers. A fisherman who was engaged in this quest was given such a blow, that after running for a few hundred metres calling for help, alerting shepherds nearby, he fell dead. The dwarf haunts the area to this day, and it is said that he has the power to stop the engines of motor vehicles. Local people have erected shrines in the vicinity, in the hope that they might avoid meeting him.[53]

In the haunted forest of Chrysovalanti, in the Agrapha, the ghosts of brigands who buried their treasure beneath the trees are said to roam the pathways, jumping out and frightening to death unwary travellers.[54]

In the area of Leonidi, Jews were said to guard treasures.[55] At Palaiokastro, Imvros, a treasure was said to be guarded by a long-haired black dog, which, when it barks, sends out sparks from its teeth.[56]

[1] Πολίτη, 1.161.

[2] Πολίτη, 1. 161.

[3] Καλέμης 419-21; Sapouria-Sakellaraki.

[4] Πολίτη, 1.162-3

[5] Πολίτη, 1:162.

[6] Abbott.

[7] Καμπούρογλου (1920) 76-7.

[8] Πολίτη, 1:52.

[9] Lee (1951)

[10] Πολίτη, 1:244.

[11] Rodd 170.

[12] Πολίτη 1:181.
[13] Πολίτη 1:190.
[14] Lawson 277.
[15] Rodd, 186.
[16] Bent, 48.
[17] Τσικλίδης (2) 2:177.
[18] Τσικλίδης (1) 2:72.
[19] Πολίτες 1:363-4.
[20] Τσικλίδης (1) 2:53-4.
[21] Τσικλίδης (1) 2:54-5.
[22] Πολίτης 1:367-8.
[23] Πολίτης 1:161.
[24] Τσικλίδης (2) 2:283-6.
[25] Τσικλίδης (2) 2:286.
[26] Τσικλίδης (2) 2:285.
[27] Τσικλίδης (2) 2:284.
[28] Τσικλίδης (2) 2:50.
[29] Τσικλίδης (2) 1:285.
[30] Caernarvon 68-9.
[31] Πολίτης 1:160.
[32] Πολίτης 1:159.
[33] Πολίτης 1:159.
[34] Θρακιώτης 301.
[35] Πολίτης 2:409.
[36] Τσικλίδης (2) 2:178.
[37] Νουάρος 1:247.
[38] Πολίτης 2:216.
[39] Blum & Blum,101.
[40] Καρασούτας 445.
[41] Πολίτη 1:178.
[42] Νουάρου 235.
[43] Θεοδοσιάδης (4) 97.
[44] Τσικλίδης (2) 2:139.
[45] Πολίτη 2:206.
[46] Πολίτη 2:206.
[47] Πολίτη 2:206.
[48] Θεοδοσιάδης (4) 96.
[49] Πολίτη 1:176.
[50] Καρατσούτας 448.
[51] Tomkinson (1) 53.
[52] Θεοδοσιάδης (4) 96-7.
[53] Τσικλίδες (2) 1:247-8.
[54] Γιαννουλάκης (1) 307.
[55] Κωστάκης 85.
[56] Θεοδοσιάδης (4) 97.

The Haunted Seas

Few professions are as uncertain and dangerous as those conducted on the sea. The fisherman and sailor have to contend with the potentially treacherous forces of wind and waves. To the summer visitor, Homer's "wine-dark" sea impresses by its beauty and friendliness. In the Aegean, in particular, one is hardly ever out of sight of land. Yet that selfsame sea is dotted with submerged mountain peaks and reefs - lurking snares for unlucky or careless sailors. The winds can be fickle and strong, and violent storms can arise without warning. At such times, the comforting presence of islets is transformed into the danger of being wrecked on inhospitable rocks.

Fishermen seek to secure their safety by having their new boats blessed by a priest. Every year, on the day of *Theophania* (Epiphany), the bishops go down to the shore and bless the waters, throwing in a cross. Each boat contains flowers from the *epitafio*, the funeral bier of the dead Christ, carried in procession on the evening of Good Friday. They also contain icons of the *Panayia*, Mary, the Mother of God, or of Saint Nicholas, the current guise of the ancient sea-god Poseidon. Few harbours lack a harbourside chapel dedicated to this patron of all who travel by sea.

The original nereids were sea nymphs. The *Iliad* mentions that there were thirty-four of them, and Hesiod fifty. They dwelt in the depths of the sea and entertained their father, Nereus, with song and dance.

In modern Greece, sea nymphs were rare. But in Thrace there were nymphs who lived in the sea, near to land, who would emerge after darkness fell, and dance on the shore by the light of the moon until cock-crow. They were believed to be dumb, with the ability to make only inarticulate noises.[1] At Mylos in the Argolid a nereid with green hair, which she decorated with pearls and coral, used to come up out of the sea. During the night she would dance in the shallow waters by the light of the moon.[2] The seas off Anaphi, when Theodore Bent visited, during the mid-nineteenth century, were particularly infested with sea-nereids, who carried on a ceaseless war with the nereids of the land.[3] In Lakonia it was best not to swim on the feast of the Transfiguration of the Saviour (August 6th), because on that day the sea was thick with nereids.[4]

In many parts of the world people believed in mermaids: hybrid creatures which inhabited the sea, with the body of a woman from the waist up, and the tail of a fish, or sometimes two, from the waist down. The Bay of Elounda was said to be haunted by a mermaid. She was probably Britomartis, who in Cretan myth was said to be a mermaid goddess, a daughter of Zeus. Known also as Dictynna, Britomartis was the almost certainly original form of the mermaid goddess Aphaia, to whom the beautiful temple on the island of Aegina was dedicated. The island of Syme, by contrast, boasted a large, long-haired, man-eating mermaid.[5]

The experience of one seaman anchored at Souda Bay in Crete, reported below, suggested to him a natural explanation for the origin of such stories.

"Early one calm summer's morning, when we were lying at anchor off the Tuzla Scala, at the head of Suda Bay, and the surface of the bay was like a mirror, the officers and men then on board were suddenly attracted by something unusual that was seen splashing and apparently sporting upon the surface of its waters at no great distance from them, and to naked eyes looked remarkably like a human head and neck, with long flowing tresses, which, from its action, the creature seemed to be occasionally throwing and tossing about from side to side, or beating upon the surface of the then calm bay, as if to free them from their entanglement, or from the matted weed they had caught up from the rocky recesses of the deep whence the strange creature had come. A mermaid, truly might easily have been the exclamation and belief of many who saw it, had they lived a century or two earlier.

And what was this phenomenon? Is the natural inquiry. Merely a common seal that was disappointing a Cretan gentleman of a delicacy of the deep; for it was breakfasting upon a huge *octopodia*, or species of eight-armed sepia or cuttlefish, with which it had risen from the bottom and come to the surface to free itself from the long tenacious arms which the strong and muscular creature had entwined round the head, face, and shoulders of the amphibian; and as these arms are each provided with large cup-like suckers, the *octopodia's* strength of hold is such that it could easily drown a man with two or three of them only, if the rest were firmly attached to a stone or rock at the bottom. Hence the seal's struggles and splashing to detach them.

When the seal had tired out by wounding, or half-drowned its victim in the air by remaining sufficiently long at the surface, it then leisurely and apparently playfully tossed and turned it over and over as a cat does a mouse; and thus represented to a distant observer all the fanciful attitudes of a mermaid in sport, or in the act of clearing her tresses from entanglements.

What more is wanting to explain the origin of mermaids, or perhaps even that of the fable of the Sirens of Aptera, over whose bath or pool we have been induced for a moment here to pause and to contemplate?

The daughters of Nereus, the ancient sea god, the Nereides—or Dorides, as they were also called—numbered, according to one account, fifty, to another, a hundred. They dwelt in a splendid cave at the bottom of the sea, and rode on dolphins or other creatures of the deep. Like all nymphs, the Nereides were playful, given to splashing about in the water, swimming, or sitting on rocks at the sea's edge, drying their wonderful tresses. It may be from them that the legend of mermaids sprung."[6]

Peculiar to Greece was the *Gorgona*, a large mermaid whose visage was sometimes fatally beautiful and sometimes hideous. She was often pictured as holding a trident and riding a dolphin, or drawn in a coach drawn by dolphins.[7] The *Gorgona* haunted the stormier parts of the sea, especially the Black Sea and the Eastern Aegean, and was particularly likely to be encountered around midnight on Saturday nights.

She was the sister of Alexander the Great. At one time, he possessed the water of life in a glass, but she spilled it after he killed the dragon which guarded it, and so he cursed her, turning her into a semi-fish. Yet she did not hold a grudge against him, for she understood her fault.

When she appeared to sailors at sea, she would seize the boat and stop its progress with her hand. She would then demand of the captain, "Does King Alexander live?" If he replied, "He lives and conquers" she would calm the winds and waves, and play beautiful music on her lyre. If he made the fatal mistake of telling her that Alexander was dead, she would become enraged, agitate the sea and sink the ship, drowning all its crew and cargo.[8]

In Thrace, this creature was known as Phokia, and thought of as the mother, rather than the sister, of Alexander the Great; but she behaved in every way as the *Gorgona.*[9]

The *Gorgones* of classical mythology were three powerful winged creatures: the mortal Medousa, and her two immortal sisters Stheno and Euryale. They were depicted as women with faces were so hideous that a glimpse of them would turn a man to stone. They had the skin of vipers, wide staring eyes, swines' tusks, red lolling tongues, flaring nostrils, short coarse beards, and their hair consisted of serpents. They were armed with sharp claws of bronze and golden wings. Clearly, the modern *Gorgona* bears little or no relation to her ancient namesakes.[10] Closer to her perhaps were the sirens. Although they were originally represented in ancient art as birds, from the fifth century AD they were depicted as whores with a fearful visage, and with the lower body of a fish.

Certainly, behind the story of the modern *Gorgona* lies the myth of Glaukos. He was a fisherman from Boioteia. One day he had drawn in his nets to land, and had taken a great many fish of various kinds, which he emptied, and began to sort out on the grass. Suddenly the fish began to revive and move their fins as if they were in the water; and while he looked on astonished, they all moved off to the edge of the river, plunged in, and swam away. He did not know what to make of this. He gathered some of the grass in that place and tasted it. He had hardly done so, than he found himself longing to enter the water, and plunged in. The gods of the water received him, and decreed that all that was mortal in him should be washed away. Soon found himself changed, both in appearance and in mind. His hair had become sea-green, and trailed behind him on the water; his shoulders grew broad, and what had been his thighs and legs took the form of a fish's tail.

One day Glaucus saw the beautiful Scylla rambling on the shore. He fell in love with her, and showing himself on the surface, spoke to her, saying such things as he thought most likely to win her heart, but Scylla would not listen to him, and hastened away. Glaucus was in despair, but he decided to consult the enchantress Circe. She told him that he should pursue someone more willing to accept his advances, but he insisted that he loved Scylla alone. So Circe took poisonous plants and mixed them together, with incantations and charms. Then she went to the coast of Sicily, where Scylla lived, and there, in a bay to which Scylla used to resort in the heat of the day, the goddess poured her poisonous mixture, and muttered over it incantations of great power. Scylla plunged into the water up to her waist. Then to her horror she saw a brood of serpents surrounding her! At first she tried to drive them away, and then to run from them, but as she ran she carried them with her, and when she tried to touch her limbs, she found her hands touch only the yawning jaws of monsters. So Scylla remained rooted to the spot. Her temper grew as ugly as her appearance, and she began to take pleasure in devouring hapless mariners who came within her grasp.

It seems likely that the modern Gorgona was originally Scylla. Then, during the Byzantine period, she came to be identified as a sister of Alexander the Great, and with the myth of the loss of the water of immortality.[11]

Waterspouts were once considered a variety of sea *lamia*. Sailors would try to protect themselves from them by thrusting the blade of their black-handled knife into the mast of their ship or boat.[12] In some places, the *lamies* of the sea were many. They would sing and dance on the waves, leaping high into the air, especially enjoying rough seas. Like the sirens of old, they would lure sailors on by their songs and voices, tricking them into thinking they were near to land, and leading them to their doom.[13] In a curious, but by no means untypical, crossing of boundaries, stories from Elis, in the north-western Peloponnese identified the *lamia* of the sea with the queen of the nereids, who lived on a mountain in Arcadia overlooking the sea. From there she would issue to attack ships with whirlwinds and waterspouts.[14]

On Parnassos it was believed that any handsome young man playing the flute by the seashore would be approached by the *lamia*, who would seek, with promises of a future happy life, to get him to accompany her into the sea. She would immediately kill him if he refused; while if he obeyed, and followed her into the depths, he would be drowned.[15]

It should come as no surprise to the reader that sea monsters of various kinds haunted the shores of Greece.

Some of these may have been entirely natural denizens of the deep, although perhaps unusual and remarkable for their size. In the mouth of a cave some distance from Ayia Pachi, on the island of Syros, is the small chapel of Ayios Stefanos. Some fishermen were once at work in the neighbourhood of the cave when they saw a huge creature below them in the water. They quickly made a vow to the saint to build him a chapel inside the cave if they were able to get safely to land, which they did. The present chapel is the result of their vow.[16]

Off Mount Himaras in Epiros sailors used to offer salt to appease a monster called the Lingeta, but they were much too afraid to explain to researchers exactly what it was.[17] Off the east coast of Samothrace lies a sunken city. The area is rich in sponges, but sponge divers feared to dive there after one of their number was eaten by a sea monster which haunted the place.[18]

Near Lagana in Zakynthos, a beast with terrifying eyes, half fish and half serpent, was believed to haunt subterranean caverns on the coast. Although essentially a sea creature, it could leave the water and drag itself about on land, which it would sometimes do. It was said to destroy those who had sold themselves to the devil for money or women.[19]

Stories from the small island of Anghistri, just off Aegina, in the Saronic Gulf, mentioned small diaphanous humanoid creatures, with membranes joining their fingers, which emerged from the sea.[20]

A folk tale from Zakynthos seems to preserve the memory of the ancient sea god Poseidon in his original form: A king who was the strongest man of his time made war on a neighbouring ruler. The secret of the king's strength lay in three hairs which grew on his breast. He was on the point of crushing his foes when his wife was bribed to cut off those hairs, and so he, with thirteen companions, was taken prisoner. After he had been incarcerated for some time, the hairs began to grow again, and so his enemies threw him and his companions into a pit. The others were all killed by the fall, but he, being thrown in last, fell upon their bodies and was saved. His enemies raised a mound over the pit. But the king found a dead bird at the bottom of the shaft, and having fastened its wings to his hands, flew up and burst through the mound. He soared high into the air until a storm of rain washed away the clay that held the feathers to his hands, and he fell into the sea. "Then from out the sea came the god thereof, and struck him with a three-pronged fork, and changed him into a dolphin until such time as he should find a maiden ready to be his wife." The dolphin, after some time saved a shipwrecked king and his daughter, and the princess, as a reward, took him for her husband, so that the spell was broken.[21]

Certainly the "demon of the sea" of Zakynthos, half man and half fish, with his trident and his dolphin steeds, is recognizably Poseidon. He was said to sleep on gold, since whatever sank into the sea was his.[22] Similarly, the inhabitants of Santorini and the neighbouring islands feared the "Warrior of the Sea" (*thalassomachos*), who was said to struggle with the fishermen to prevent them fishing, and tried to take their catches from them. He would call up the winds, and in this way hinder their work. Perhaps in this "Warrior of the Sea" we can again recognise the hostile aspect of the ancient sea-god.[23]

[1] Θρακιώτης 299.

[2] Τσικλίδες (2) 1:226.

[3] Bent 48.

[4] Stewart 279.

[5] Χατζηδάκη.

[6] Spratt 133-4.

[7] Καμηλάκη.

[8] Χατζηδάκη.

[9] Καμηλάκη.

[10] Κουνενάκη.

[11] Χατζηδάκη.

[12] Bent 71.

[13] Πολίτης 1:368-9.

[14] Πολίτης 1:368; Lawson 172.

[15] Lawson 172.

[16] Καμηλάκη 10.

[17] Πολίτης 1:229.

[18] Πολίτης 1:229.

[19] Πολίτης 1:228.
[20] Τσικλίδες (1) 1:190.
[21] Lawson. 75.
[22] Πολίτης 1:225.
[23] Βούρνας και Γαρίδη 38.

The Spirits of Christmas

Most of the *xotika* of Greek folk tradition have some parallels in other cultures. Almost unique to the Greeks and Turks, however, were the goblins called *kallikantzaroi* which were believed to infest of the land during the twelve nights of Christmas.

They were swarthy, naked, half-human, half-animal, hairy beings, with huge heads, glaring red eyes, their blood-red tongues perpetually hanging out, goats' or asses' ears, ferocious tusks, monkeys' arms, and long curved nails, and the legs of an ass or goat, with cloven hooves. Sometimes they are represented with only one leg like that of a goat or an ass, but more commonly both are those of animals. Most were small, but a few were several metres tall. These latter were black and shaggy, with outsize bald heads and outsize male organs.[1]

These demonic creatures emerged on Christmas Eve, and remained at large for the twelve nights of Christmas, disappearing into the earth on the eve of the Epiphany, when across the country the priests go from house to house sprinkling holy water as a blessing.

They were seen as ranging in character from mischievous and tricky to extremely dangerous. During the twelve nights of Christmas they would issue from the caves where they spent the days feasting on toads, lizards, and suchlike, and would pester people in various ways. They would rush about in the darkness, bruising and trampling all who got in their way, breaking into mills, eating some of the flour and fouling the rest by defecating on it. In houses, they would break furniture, eat and drink the food, and defecate all over the place. However, they might carry good-looking women back to their caves, and even try to kill people by choking them in their beds at night, by sitting on their chests, leaving them half suffocated and nearly dead with fright. In Crete, they were believed to carry cradles of thorns on their backs into which they would put babies they had stolen, to carry them back to their caves and drink their blood.[2] Sometimes the *kallikantzaroi* would go up into the hills, to the shepherds sitting around their fires, to get warm. Not infrequently, shepherds would come down from the mountains suffering from burns when they scattered the coals.[3]

During the period they remained above ground, people would keep their houses closed up throughout the night, for fear they should get inside. In order to avoid being bothered, people would scratch a cross on their doors. In some areas, a pot of rue strategically placed by the front door of the house, or the lower jaw of a pig hung behind the door, was supposed to have a similar effect. Hanging a sieve or a bundle of flax outside the door was calculated to keep the would-be intruders busy counting until cockcrow. But mostly, in an odd parallel to the Western Santa Claus, the unwelcome visitors would get in by way of the chimney. For this reason, people would keep their hearths alight continuously throughout this period. They would also take care to throw onto the fire branches which would crackle and bang, so as to frighten away their unwelcome visitors, or old shoes to accomplish the same by an unwholesome stench. That lower jaw of a dead pig could also be employed to safeguard the family against intruders via the chimney[4] If a *kallikantzaros* found the fire out, he would urinate on it, and it would never be possible to light a decent fire in that place again.[5]

Hot coals were dropped into the wells and burnt sticks laid across them in order to keep the *kallikantzaroi* from defiling them. Those who chanced to have a black cock were considered safe, for the *kallikantzaroi* had a mortal aversion to this animal.[6] In northern Greece bonfires were lit in the towns and villages, people would sing Christmas carols around them, and ring the sheep and goat bells in order to drive them away.[7]

Luckily, the *kallikantzaroi* were not very intelligent, and were easily deceived. Many anecdotes demonstrate how they could be outwitted. A traditional piece of advice is that when a *kallikantzaros* asks, as he will if you meet him, "Will you have tow of me or lead?" you have only to answer, "Tow," and his influence is gone. Again, you should hand a sieve to him, whereupon he will set to work to count the holes. As he cannot count beyond two, this will take him until the morning, when he will have to flee.[8]

An Athenian story told of a trick played upon them by a woman whom they came upon out of doors one night, and whose bread they wanted to steal. She agreed to go with them into her house, but suggested that she would first tell them a story. It was a long one, and during the telling the first cock crowed. "Black!" said the goblins, "we are not afraid of you." By this they meant that it was still night. As she proceeded with her story, a second cock crowed. "Red!" they cried, "we are not afraid of you either." At that time, it was nearing dawn. But before the story was ended the third cock crowed. "White!" they screamed, meaning that it was day, and ran off, leaving the woman safe.[9]

Other anecdotes carry the same message: "One Christmas Day when everybody had gone to church, a single woman was left behind in her home cooking. As she was frying some liver, she saw a small disfigured child spring up in front of her. It began to grow in size and to jump around her, before asking her what her name was. She was clever enough to reply, "I, myself." The *kallikantzaros*, for such it was, continued to tease her. When her chance came, the woman turned the pan upside down, and threw it, and the burning oil which was in it, over the creature. He screamed with pain and rushed outside, where a gang of his fellows were waiting for him. "Who burned you?" they all asked. "I, myself," screamed the scalded creature. Then the others teased him, telling him that he deserved his pain for having been so stupid as to burn himself. Thus, using a trick employed by no less a predecessor than Odysseus himself, the woman was saved.[10]

Mills seem to have been a particular target of the *kallikantzaroi*. They would break in, tie up the miller, gagging him with faeces, eat the corn and flour, and urinate and defecate on the rest.[11]

Once upon the eve of Epiphany a man of Skyros was returning home from a mill late at night, driving his mule before him laden with two sacks of meal. When he had gone about halfway, he saw in front of him some *kallikantzaroi* in the road. Realising his danger, he at once got upon his mule and laid himself flat between the two sacks and covered himself up with a rug, so as to look like another sack of meal. In minutes the *kallikantzaroi* were swarming about his mule. As he held his breath he heard them saying, "Here is a pack on this side and a pack on that side, and the top-load in the middle, but where is the man?" So they ran back to the mill thinking that he had loitered behind; but they could not find him and came back after the mule, and looked again, and said, "Here is a pack on this side and a pack on that side, and the top-load in the middle, but where is the man?" So they ran on in front fearing that he had hurried on home before his mule. But when they could not find him, they returned again, and repeated what they had said before, going back to the mill a second time. This happened many times. Now as they were running to and fro, the mule was nearing home, and when the beast stopped at the door of the man's house, the *kallikantzaroi* were close to discovering him. The man therefore called quickly to his wife. She opened the door and he slipped inside, but the mule was left standing outside the house. Then the *kallikantzaroi* realised that he had tricked them, and they knocked at the door in anger. The woman, fearing lest they would break in by force, promised to open to them on condition that they should first count for her the holes in her sieve. To this they agreed, and she let it down to them by a cord from a window. Immediately they set to work to count, and counted round and round the outermost circle and never got nearer to the middle; nor could they discover how this happened, but only counted more and more hurriedly, without advancing at all. Meanwhile dawn was breaking, and as soon as the neighbours saw the *kallikantzaroi* they hurried off and fetched the priests. They immediately set out, armed with censers and holy-water vessels, to chase the *kallikantzaroi* away. Right through the town the imps fled, spreading havoc in their path and hotly pursued by the priests. At last when they were clear of the town, one *kallikantzaros* began to fall behind, and with a great effort the leading priest caught up with him and struck him on the hinder foot with his sprinkling vessel. The foot fell off, but the *kallikantzaros* fled, maimed though he was. And thus that spot came to be known as "the *Kallikantzaros'* foot."[12]

A tale also used to be told in various versions on Skyros, of a girl sent by her wicked stepmother to a mill during the dangerous Twelve Nights, ostensibly to get some corn ground, but really in the hope that she would fall prey to the *kallikantzaroi*. Having arrived at the mill the girl called in vain to the miller to help unload her mule, and entering in search of him she found him bound to his chair, apparently dead with fright, and a number of *kallikantzaroi* standing about him. They at once seized the girl, and began to quarrel among themselves which should have her for his own. But the girl kept her wits, and said that she would willingly become the wife of the one who brought her the best bridal array. So they dispersed in search of fine clothing and jewellery. Meanwhile she set to work to grind the corn, and each time a *kallikantzaros* returned with presents, she sent him on a fresh errand for something more. Finally the corn was all ground, and she quickly loaded the mule with two sacks, one on either side, clothed herself in the gold and jewels which the *kallikantzaroi* had already brought, mounted the mule, and lay flat on the saddle covered over with a sack. Eluding the *kallikantzaroi,* who pursued her, she reached home in safety. Her wicked stepmother, seeing that her plans had miscarried, and that her stepdaughter was now rich while her own daughter remained poor, determined to send her on the next evening to the mill. She too found the mill occupied by the gang of *kallikantzaroi*, but not being as shrewd as her half-sister, she was stripped of her own clothes, dressed in the skin of her mule, which the *kallikantzaroi* had killed and flayed, and sent her home with a necklace of the mule's entrails around her neck.[13]

Surprisingly, considering their bestial character and lawless nature, the *kallikantzaroi* could sometimes be shocked by the behaviour of humans. Two women from near Kalamata once went to a distant spring to collect water, and because it was late when they got there, decided to spend the night at a threshing floor. In the middle of the night, the *kallikantzaroi* came and danced there. They found the women and made them join in their dance. These old women were not of good character. They took off all their clothes, and then joined in the dance in such an uninhibited manner that the *kallikantzaroi* were shocked, and hurriedly left without bothering them further.[14]

Despite the humorous character of many of these stories, others show that in some areas the *kallikantzaroi* were considered to be very dangerous.

Three women on Spetses were once gathering wood by the sea when one of their number disappeared, and all efforts to find the missing woman proved unavailing. Then, some days later, on sailing past that part of the coast, some sailors saw her standing, alone and dazed, on some rocks by the shore. They put in and took her on board, and dropped her off in the town. After her ordeal she was dumb, and unable to explain what had happened to her. Only after an exorcism in a church was she able to speak. When she did so, she revealed that she had been kidnapped by the *kallikantzaroi*.[15]

On New Year's Eve, a shepherd was walking to the sheep pen rather late one night. He had been delayed because his mother was late in baking the sweet cakes he was carrying with him. When the *kallikantzaroi* met him, they kept asking him different questions and teasing him. The shepherd knew that if he spoke to them, he would be lost. He also knew that if he had some gunpowder to explode, they would disappear, but unfortunately, he did not have any either. Anyway, the shepherd did his best not to utter a word, even though they kept on teasing him. Finally, he got so irritated at them that he swore: "Go to the devil." That was all they needed. They jumped on him and killed him.[16]

A story known in varying forms all over Greece, introduces us to the domestic circle of a *kallikantzaros*. A midwife was roused one night during the Christmas period by a furious rapping at her door, and, imagining that the call was urgent, slipped on her clothes in haste without enquiring who it was that needed her services. Stepping out of her door found herself face to face with a stranger who asked her to accompany him to his home. On the way, as he told her that the child to which his wife was about to give birth had to be male, she realised that he was a *kallikantzaros*. He said that if it were a boy he would reward her handsomely. If turned out to be a female, he explained that he would devour the midwife. When they arrived at the cave where the *kallikantzaroi* dwelt, the midwife went about her task, and the wife of the *kallikantzaros* was soon delivered of a child; but to the midwife's horror it was female. Her wits however did not desert her, and she quickly devised a scheme to escape the shortly-to-be-enraged father. Taking a candle, she warmed it and fashioned from the wax a model of the male organs, and fastened it to the child. Then calling the *kallikantzaros*, she told him that a fine male child had been born and held up the infant for him to see. He was overjoyed, and told her to swaddle it. When she had done this, she asked to return home. The happy *kallikantzaros*, true to his word, rewarded her with a sack of gold and let her go.[17]

At the *Theophania* (Epiphany or Twelfth Night), the priest goes round to bless the houses, the wells, and the fountains, sprinkling them with holy water. At that time, the *kallikantzaroi* would return to the bowels of the earth singing. Once there, they would set to work trying to saw through the trunk of the great tree by which the ground is supported.[18] In Dimitsana, it was said that it is not a tree, but three huge wooden columns, which uphold the world, and which the *kallikantzaroi* ceaselessly seek to cut down.[19]

In Crete, infants born at Christmas were said to become *kallikantzaroi*, punishment for the sin of their parents, for impiously conceiving, and sacrilegiously bringing a child into the world, on the days on which Christ himself was conceived and born; while in Zakynthos, Christmas Eve alone was the forbidden time.[20] On Chios, all children born between Christmas and New Year's Day were doomed to this fate.[21] Measures taken by parents to prevent the development of children born during this period into *kallikantzaroi* included binding in straw or garlic tresses, or singeing the toenails; for a child without toenails could not become a *kallikantzaros*.[22]

The *yialoudes* of Santorini were a unique species of female *kallikantzaroi*. They were girls who born on Christmas Day, especially during that period of time when the gospel of the day is read in the churches. When they grew up, they would take to sleepwalking at night during the period between Christmas and Epiphany. Whoever met them walking abroad, especially near a spring, had to awaken them, or they could drown them without realising what they were doing.[23] On Paros the *kalkagari* would torment their friends with their sleepwalking. This could be prevented only with a blessed palm nailed above the door.[24]

An incredible amount of ink has been employed in trying to ascertain the origin of these strange creatures, almost unique to Greek folklore.

It has been suggested by some that the *kallikantzaroi* were nothing more than a personification of the nightmares brought on by indigestion during the twelve days of feasting during the holiday season. This seems a particularly feeble attempt at explanation for so a lively and widespread a belief in creatures who were feared as posing a real threat to the good order of the home and the safety of its inhabitants.

Folklorist George A. Megas considered that they had some connection with the souls of the dead, who in ancient times were believed to live in the underworld, and to return to the surface of the earth for a period each year when Hades opened its gates during the festival of the Anthesteria.[25] This theory, however, does justice neither to their appearance nor to the time of year when they roamed abroad.

It is possible that they were connected with the werewolf, a man who is supposed to change into a wolf. In southern Greece the *kallikantzaroi* were sometimes known as *lycanthropoi*, or "man wolves," while it has been conjectured by Bernhard Schmidt that the name *"kallikantzaros"* derives from two Turkish words meaning "black" and "werewolf."

In an attempt to reconcile conflicting evidence, J. C. Lawson, in his *Modern Greek Folklore and Ancient Greek Religion,* claimed to detect two quite different classes of *kallikantzaroi* in the tradition: one he identified with ordinary werewolves, while the other, hairy, clawed demons, he connected, rather unconvincingly, with centaurs. Although the centaurs of classical mythology were creatures with the lower bodies of horses and the upper bodies of men, Patrick Leigh Fermor points out that the centaur of classical mythology was a late idealization of a much older tradition, in which centaurs were simply human animal hybrids, which could appear in many varieties, and could be either quadrupeds or bipeds.[26]

However, by far the most plausible explanation offered so far seems to be that of folklorist Nicholas Polites, who argued that these strange creatures are derived from the once common practice of masquerading during the midwinter festival season. At roughly this time of the year, the ancient Greeks celebrated the Chronia, and the Rural Dionysia. Under Roman rule, it was the Saturnalia, Brumalia and Kalandae which were celebrated, although the actual festivities observed probably changed little in character from their by that time traditional form. During these celebrations, people dressed up in masks and animal costumes, and went around playing tricks on people, intimidating them, and behaving in a riotous manner, and there was a lot of drinking. There is even evidence of human sacrifice at this time. These mummers were the successors of the *silenoi*, or satyrs, who, in ancient times attended the revels of the god Dionysos. In parts of northern and central Greece, such traditions have been preserved up to the present time.[27] Polites considered that the figure of the *kallikantzaros* was suggested by these bizarrely dressed revellers.[28] There is a lot of evidence to support this view.

The tradition of the Teniotes was that the *kallikantzaroi* were not *xotika* at all, but humans who became crazy with the arrival of Christmas, and ran about here and there causing trouble. This was said to have been brought about by some fault in the priest's reading of the rite when they were baptized, which rendered it invalid.[29] This strongly suggests that the *kallikantzaroi* were originally a satirical depiction, the product of a jaundiced viewpoint, of the revellers of the Midwinter festivities.

In some parts of Greece, the *kallikantzaroi* were called *pagana*, a term which in Roman times referred not to worshippers of idols, but to the followers of Dionysos during the revels of the Saturnalia, Kalends, etc.[30]

Although he did not himself favour this view, George A. Megas unwittingly gave it some support when he asserted that during Epiphany

(*Theophania*): "In some parts of Greece it is the custom to masquerade and go round the village wearing hideous masks and jingling bells. Both the masks and the bells are meant to frighten away the *kallikantzaroi*. Sometimes the villagers dress up as *kallikantzaroi* and walk round the village scaring the children."[31] The unlikelihood that *both* these contrary explanations offered for the behaviour of the masqueraders could be true is obvious. Polites' view is that the second of these contentions was the correct one.

The prompt disappearance of these exotic figures with the blessing of the waters on *Theophania* (Epiphany) suggests a deliberate attempt by the church to use that festival to bring the pagan midwinter revels to an end. A similar phenomenon may be observed on the day before Clean Monday, or on Clean Monday itself, when various ceremonies were deliberately devised, such as the expulsion, burning or burying of the Carnival, or Carnival King, firmly and completely to bring the revels of the Carnival of spring to an end with the beginning of the Lenten fast.[32]

Other Greek seasonal spirits were the *drymes*, which were active during the first few days of March and August. March was once notionally the beginning of summer, and August (rather surprisingly) the beginning of winter. The first few days of each of those months, also called *drymes*, were periods when people were liable to attack. Potentially risky things like cutting wood, swimming, or leaving the children out of doors at noon, were avoided. The *drymes* particularly attacked during activities connected with water, so washing one's clothes or hair were also considered inadvisable during these periods.[33]

The *drymes* did not seem to have been visualised, and constituted nothing more than an indefinite threat.

[1] Fermor (1) 192.
[2] Rodd, 189ff.
[3] Blum & Blum, 122
[4] Megas 35.
[5] Blum & Blum, 120.
[6] Rodd, 199.
[7] Megas 36-7.
[8] Rodd, 200-1.
[9] Rodd, 201.
[10] Blum & Blum, 120.
[11] Fermor (1) 193.

[12] Περδικά 2:138-9.
[13] Περδικά 2:139.
[14] Θεοδοσιάδης 80.
[15] Rodd 199.
[16] Blum & Blum 121.
[17] Πολίτης 1:275.
[18] Rodd 197f.
[19] Θεοδοσιαδης (1) 361.
[20] Rodd 200.
[21] Πολίτης 1;242-3.
[22] Megas 35.
[23] Καναράκης 413.
[24] Bent 187.
[25] Megas 34-5.
[26] Fermor (1) 197.
[27] Tomkinson (4) 16-25.
[28] Πολίτης 2:324-43.
[29] Θεοδοσιάδης (4) 146.
[30] Λουκάτος.
[31] Megas 50.
[32] Tomkinson (4) 36.
[33] Megas 81, 147.

The Fates

It was a common belief well into the twentieth century that each person had an individual fate, something like a guardian angel, but that every person's destiny was ultimately controlled by the great trinity of Fates, known as "the Fates of all Fates." These three terrible beings were only ever mentioned using honeyed words, so as not to offend them, although at the same time, and with the typical inconsistency of folk beliefs, it was also held that they were absolutely implacable, and could never be persuaded to change their decrees.

Traditionally, on the day when a mother rose from childbed, she would remain completely silent, "lest the Fates snatch her speech." The third night of the baby's life was considered the most important, when its fortunes would be sealed for ever. At that time, the three "Fates of all the fates" were expected to visit the baby in person and to make their all-important decisions.

Elaborate preparations would be made, supervised by the midwife, to make their visit a pleasant one, and to avoid annoying them in any way. The baby would be bathed in water scented with laurel or rosemary, and then put to sleep by itself in the best room of the house. A black-handled knife, a coin or a book of the Gospels, would be placed under the pillow of a baby boy, while ornaments would be left under a girl's pillow, in an effort to influence the deliberations of the Fates. The doors which communicated with the rest of the house would be closed, while that leading to the outside door, which would be unlocked, would be kept open. All dogs would be kept securely on chains, and any obstacles over which visitors might trip in the darkness would be carefully pushed out of the way. A light would be kept burning all that night in the room where the baby was sleeping. Beside the cradle, a low table would be set out surrounded by cushions; for this was the fashion in which the Fates had traditionally been greeted, and no one would dare to risk requiring them to adapt to modern upright chairs and high tables. On the table, refreshments would be set out: usually honey, white almonds, bread, and water; perhaps with other dainties as well. The family jewels might be displayed on a side table, from which the expected visitors could take their pick if they so desired.

The Fates would arrive some time shortly after midnight. No other human might remain with the baby during that time, but listening mothers often claimed to have detected a low murmur coming from the baby's room at this time. Many stories told how a mother overheard the Fates discussing the time and manner of her child's death. It always happened that whatever the mother overheard would come true, despite the most elaborate precautions she might take to prevent it.[1]

Any marks subsequently observed on the baby's face, such as moles, especially on the brow, were called the "writing of the Fates." Despite all the best efforts to propitiate them, it was commonly said that the Fates never gave anyone an entirely good destiny.[2]

On the island of Sikinos, on the child's first birthday all the relatives would gather together to learn the baby's fate by divination. A tray would be brought in with various objects on it: a pen, a coin, a tool, an egg. Whichever object the child touched first would indicate his fortune. The worst fate was indicated by touching an egg, since this meant that the child would become a layabout.[3]

There are many folk tales the point of which is clearly to illustrate the futility of trying to avoid the inexorable decrees of the Fates.

A youth, while travelling, stopped at a peasant's cottage to spend the night. He was received hospitably, and laid himself down to sleep in a corner of the bedroom, in which his host and hostess were also sleeping. The woman had given birth to a baby girl child two days before. As the youth lay on his mattress awake in the darkness, he perceived Fate, Fortune, and Death stalk into the room in order to allot to the baby her portion in life. They glanced at the stranger and immediately walked out, but the youth heard them holding a consultation amongst themselves outside the door. At last, one of them said: "The little maid shall become the strange youth's wife," and the others agreed.

Our traveller was not at all pleased with the offhand way in which they also disposed of his own destiny. For he was an ambitious youth, and the prospect of marrying a poor peasant's daughter accorded ill with his ambitions. So, in order to avoid the fulfilment of this decree, he got up softly, stole to the baby's cradle and taking her in his arms crept out of the cottage. After going some distance, he threw her into a thorn hedge and continued on his journey, fondly confident that by his decisive actions he had thwarted Fate. Next morning the peasant and his wife discovered their loss, and went in quest of their offspring. They soon found her, unscathed, save for a scratch across her breast, which left a lifelong scar.

Years went by, and the stranger, now a prosperous man, chanced to journey that way again. Having long forgotten the episode, this time, he put up at an inn opposite the peasant's house. A fair girl appeared at the cottage window, and he was so smitten by her beauty that he forthwith stepped across the road and asked her parents for her hand in marriage. It was only after the wedding that the sight of the scar, and his bride's explanation of it, led to the discovery that she was the infant he had sought to destroy.

Sometimes, the attempt to evade the decree of the Fates proves not only fruitless, but fatal.

Once upon a time, there was a very wealthy man, rich in houses, sheep and goats. Yet, in spite of all his wealth, he was a miser. This man chanced to visit a big city, but he refrained from putting up at an inn, since that involved spending money. Nor would he go to some great man's palace, lest he should incur an obligation which he might one day be called upon to reciprocate. Instead, he stopped at a poor man's cottage. The house was only one big room and the hall, and they put him up in a corner of the room. His servant had to make do in the yard with the horses.

Now, the poor man's wife had been delivered of a boy which was three days old when this wealthy man arrived. So they laid them down to sleep in the evening, the guest in one corner of the room and the woman in child-bed with her husband in the other. These went to sleep at once, and slept soundly. But sleep would not seize on the wealthy man. He turned now on this side, now on the other, trying to calculate how to augment his wealth. While he was thinking, all of a sudden he saw the door thrown open, and in came three women clad in white. They were the Fates. They entered the room and stood where the little one lay sleeping. One of the Fates touched him with her finger and said: " What kind of destiny shall we allot him? " Another answered: "Let us make him heir to the wealthy man who is lying over there in the corner." "Agreed," said the others. Thus they decreed and vanished. The wealthy man heard these words and was afraid, and now could not sleep from fear. He rose and began to pace up and down in the room until daybreak.

With first light, when the poor man rose from bed, the visitor said to him: " I am going home today. I have no children of my own. If you will give me your baby, my wife and I will bring it up just as if it were our own flesh and blood. You are young and, please God, you can have more children." Thereupon the poor man called to his wife to see what she had to say, and she at first would not consent, but at length, lest they should spoil the child's chance of good fortune, she answered, "Very well," and consented to give it away, although she loved it as a mother should. She suckled it well until it had enough milk, then she dressed it in the best clothes she had, and kissed it crosswise on the forehead. The wealthy man took the child, saddled his horse, was bidden "God speed" and went away with his servant.

When they got outside the city and reached a lonely place in the midst of the standing corn, for it was summer, the rich man reined in his mare and said to his servant: "Take this baby and kill it with a stone." The servant at first would not do it, for he was a God-fearing man; but finally, he made as if to obey his master. He took up the baby, but instead of striking the child, he struck the earth with a stone, so that his master thought that he had struck the child. Then he suddenly made as though he saw someone approaching from afar, ran to his horse, pretending to be frightened, and made off as speedily as he could. And so he left the little one sleeping among the ears of corn.

Those fields happened to belong to a rich farmer who had no children of his own, and both his wife and he had frequently prayed that God might give them one. Then, despairing of that, they had wished to adopt a child. On that evening, the farmer happened to be strolling in the fields and heard the child crying. He walked towards the voice, and by and by, he came across the little one. As it was pretty and clean, he took a fancy to it and carried it to his wife. "Look what I have found in the fields, wife," said he. "We wished for a child and God has sent one to us." His wife was doubtful. "Who knows who is the child's mother?" she said. "But, I do not mind. Let us keep it." They decided to keep it and hired a nurse to suckle it, and when it grew up, they sent it to school. The boy made progress and was very fond of them, and they in their turn were fond of him, and they called him Naïdis, or "Foundling."

Time went by, and Naïdis became sixteen or seventeen years old. Then, one day the wicked wealthy man who had tried to kill him when he was a baby chanced to visit the very house where he lived. He heard the people call the boy Naïdis, and he was surprised at the strangeness of the name. He enquired of his hostess why they had given him such a strange name. " . . . We gave him that name because he is not our own son," she explained. "My husband found him some seventeen years ago in the fields amidst the standing crops. We had no children, so we brought him up, and love him as our own, and he loves us very much indeed."

The wealthy man on hearing this was grieved at heart, for he understood that it was the child he had ordered his servant to kill. He wondered what was to be done. At length an idea occurred to him. He and said that he had a letter to send home and that he wanted a trusty man to carry it. "Why, we will send Naïdis," they answered. They prepared a cake and other food for Naïdis, and he saddled his horse. The wealthy man gave him a letter for his wife, in which he told her to send the bearer up to the mountain pastures where his flocks were grazing, and to instruct the shepherds there to cut him to pieces and fling his body into a well.

Naïdis took the letter without any suspicion, mounted his horse, and set out. But before he left, his mother advised him to take care and not to drink water when he was tired; then she kissed him and bade him Good-bye. On the way, he reached a spring under a tree, and alighted in order to rest awhile and then drink, according to his mother's advice, for he was very thirsty. As he was sitting there under the shadow of the tree, an old man with a long white beard passed by and greeted him, and asked him where he was going. The young man responded by telling him his destination and his mission. "Give me that letter that I may see it; for I think I know the man." The boy gave him the letter, and the old man passed his hand over it, returned it, and then went on his way. To cut a long story short, Naïdis arrived at the wealthy man's house towards evening. As he was dismounting, he looked up and saw a beautiful young woman standing at the window. In the twinkling of an eye, he fell in love with her. She was the wealthy man's daughter; for he had lied when he said that he had no children: he had a daughter and a son.

Naïdis entered the house, and the wealthy man's wife greeted him warmly. He delivered the letter to her. She opened it, and read as follows: "Take this youth and our daughter, summon a priest and see that they are married immediately. I am coming home eight days hence, and I must find the thing done." Having read the letter, the wife did as she thought her husband had ordered. She called in a priest and without delay had them wedded. They celebrated their wedding with much jollity and music until daybreak. Eight days afterwards the wealthy man returned, and, as he alighted and dismounted from his horse, he lifted up his eyes and saw his own daughter standing by the side of Naïdis on the balcony. Then he was seized with giddiness - like a fit of apoplexy - and fell down upon the ground. They ran and summoned the doctors, and after a great deal of trouble they managed to bring him to. When he had recovered, he said: "It was nothing. I was weary from the journey, and the sun struck me. " But why did you not do as I instructed you in my letter? " I certainly have," she replied. Here is your letter. Look and see what you wrote." He took the letter and read it. He thought that he was dreaming. He rubbed his eyes again and again, but could not make out how it had happened; for it was his clearly in his own hand. Then he said: "Very well, it does not matter. Tomorrow you must call Naïdis at dawn and send him up to the flocks with a letter which I will give you."

He sat down and wrote another letter to his shepherds saying the same as before.

Next morning, very early, his wife got up and went to call Naïdis. But when she entered into the room and saw him sleeping sweetly in her daughter's arms, she was reluctant to wake him, and let him sleep on for another hour. Instead, she went to her own son and said: "Are you still asleep, my boy? " "No, mother," he replied "Get your horse and take this letter to the shepherds who tend the flocks," she said. The boy got up, mounted his horse, took the letter, and set out. After a while her husband also got up and asked her: " Have you sent him?" "I was reluctant to wake Naïdis," she answered, "but it does not matter, my husband, I sent your letter with our own son." "What have you done, woman?" he cried, and he rushed out like someone possessed to overtake his son. Alarmed, his wife rushed after him. When the rich man reached his shepherds, he discovered that they had already slain his son, and thrown his body down a deep well. Mad with grief and remorse, he threw himself into the well and perished. His wife arrived just behind him, and seeing her husband throw himself into the well, she lost her senses and threw herself into it as well, and also died. Thus Naïdis became the heir of the rich man.

The informant in Thessaloniki who told this story to G. F. Abbott in the middle of the twentieth century added that this was not a mere fairy tale; but that it demonstrated that no one can escape his fate.[4]

One girl on Naxos did not to so badly in changing her destiny. Excessively ugly, she managed to find out from a magician where the Fates lived, and that if she could get them to eat salt, she could also get them to change her fate. She somehow succeeded in all this, became very beautiful and married a prince, but she never had any children. So even she satisfied the traditional belief that the Fates never allow anyone to be altogether happy.[5]

In nineteenth century Athens, when a girl reached the period shortly before marriage, or if any marriage at all was beginning to be despaired of, her mother would become uneasy once again. Rather inconsistently, it was believed that the role of the Fates would again become crucial in deciding the fortunes of a young woman. A plate would be prepared with spoonfuls of honey and taken to one of the many caves of the Fates in the neighbourhood by an old woman who was either a member of the family, or who was trusted by them. She had to be freshly bathed and wear a new dress. It was important that she should also take with her myrrh and incense; otherwise, the Fates would not accept her offering. She would leave the offerings and return to the cave on the next day. If the honey had disappeared, it signified that the Fates had accepted her offering and the girl's future good fortune was assured. If the offering were partly consumed, then good fortune would come in time. If it had been ignored entirely, the old woman would sing a dirge in the face of the poor girl's evil destiny.[6]

The English visitor Christopher Dodwell wrote that the cave known mistakenly as "Socrates' Prison" on the Hill of the Pnyx was still used for such offerings in his day. He found "in the inner chamber, a small feast consisting of a cup of honey and white almonds, a cake on a little napkin, and a vase of aromatic herbs burning, and exhaling an agreeable perfume." He records that his donkey ate some of the offering, insensible of the pleasure its action would give the girl on whose behalf they had been deposited. On the Museion Hill several old rock dwellings in the form of caves were employed in a similar fashion.[7]

A further inconsistency is to be found in the practice of attempting to persuade the Fates to change someone's destiny by sending down a curse upon them. Thus Thomas Smart Hughes wrote:

"I was informed also of another singular custom existing amongst the lower classes, wherein these *Moirai* or Destinies are concerned. When a man of revengeful disposition has received an injury from his neighbour, and is unwilling to seek redress by the ordinary modes, he betakes himself to build up a curse in the form of a round barrow or mound of stones, laying large ones for a foundation and leaving room for his relatives or friends, or any passing traveller who may take an interest in his cause, to add a pebble to his anathema. He then solemnly calls upon the Fates to shower down every species of calamity upon the head of the offender, and not unfrequently joins the arch fiend in his energetic invocation. Sometimes it happens that an accident from the pistol of a Turk, or a malaria fever, takes off the devoted victim, very opportunely for the anathematizer, who is then regarded with reverential awe, and esteemed as a person under the special influence of divine protection: it is also thought that in most instances the corpse of the deceased becomes a *Vrucolacos*, possessed by an evil spirit, which prevents it from decaying, and engages it in every species of mischief: the only remedy for this is to disinter it, tear out the heart, and cut the body into four quarters; which being burned, the ashes are scattered to the winds."[8]

Although belief in the Fates was universal, and they were generally believed to live somewhere vaguely "in the mountains,"[9] they were especially associated with a few locations; for example, the caves on the Hill of the Pnyx in Athens, in caves on Skyros, and in the mountains of Tayetos and Pelion.[10] They were also believed to bathe in a spring at Amphissa just before dawn to wash and comb the golden hair which falls to their shoulders, suggesting that there they were believed to be beautiful. On New Year's Eve, pomegranates and sweets would be offered to them at the spring.[11] They would dance so frequently on a rock on Anghistri that they gave their name to the place.[12] Athenians regarded an ancient cave dedicated to the nymphs in Kifissia as sacred to the three Fates, who were believed not only to determine the future, but also to reveal their decisions in visions, dreams, and by other means. In 1836, Christopher Wordsworth wrote: "At Cephissia (Kifissia, in the northern suburbs of Athens) is a grotto, dedicated to the *Moirai* or Fates, to which the female peasants resort to learn thence their future destiny..." If a loose fragment fell from the vault of the grotto while they were there, it was believed that the *Moira* would be favourable towards them and they would receive good fortune. According to tradition, at one time a magus known as Tsarouchas claimed to have made a convenient arrangement with the Fates, by which, for a price, he would travel between Athens and Kifissia taking questions to them from the women of Athens, and conveying their replies back to the city.[13]

The ancient Greeks usually conceived the Fates or *Moiroi as* three ugly, terrible and merciless old women wearing veils woven out of spiders' webs, who controlled the destinies of both gods and men. Clotho, the spinner, spun the thread of a person's life; Lachesis, the apportioner sometimes portrayed as writing, decided how much time was allowed each person and recorded it; while Atropos, the inevitable, carried scissors to cut the thread when a person's apportioned time was up, at which point he died. Even the Olympian gods feared this terrible trio. By modern times, their names had been forgotten among the ordinary people, but their distinct functions were remembered.

These Greek Fates correspond to the Norns, the three Fates of northern European tradition. The widespread area covered by this belief suggests a very early origin for them. Thus here we have a direct survival, well into the twentieth century, of a belief once common to many parts of Europe; a belief which was probably already immemorially ancient in the heyday of classical Greek civilization.

[1] Πολίτης 1:413-4.

[2] e.g. Fermor (1) 183.

[3] Bent 92.

[4] Abbott 131-3.

[5] Bent 93.

[6] Hughes 298.

[7] Dodwell.

[8] Hughes 299.

[9] Bent 92-3.

[10] Fermor (1) 183.

[11] Θεοδοσιάδης 82.

[12] Τσικλίδης (1) 1:192.

[13] For a fuller account of this cave and the ancient cult associated with it, see Tomkinson (2) 54-5.

Agents of Sickness and Disease

Before the real causes of disease were understood by science, people attributed diseases, especially epidemics, to paranormal sources.

Early statistics show that infant mortality was endemic before the development of modern medicine. Even today, so-called "cot deaths" can seem mysterious and inexplicable to the bereaved parents. In consequence, young children were thought to be particularly susceptible to harm from *xotika*, and the closer to the moment of birth, the more vulnerable they were. This led to a general fear of allowing the entry of *xotika* into the house where there was either a pregnant mother or a young baby.

Scott McNall was told: "Gina Politi, returning from the fields after taking her father his lunch, walked down by the stream and heard laughter and singing coming from the pool. She ran home and tried to tell her mother, but her mother, who was pregnant, and afraid the baby would be marked, would not listen. She put a candle in the doorway so that the flame would prevent the evil spirits from following Gina into the house."[1]

The unchurched mother was not supposed to leave her baby for a moment, and a recently delivered mother was not supposed to be left alone at all, even inside the house. After darkness fell, no one besides her husband and close kin were supposed to enter the house. It was also said that two unchurched mothers should on no account ever encounter one another, not even by chance, for one of them would inevitably die.[2]

Unbaptized babies were believed to be particularly vulnerable to attack because they did not have the protection of the baptismal chrism. In many places, the clothes of unbaptized children were not left outside to dry overnight because it was believed that evil spirits would cling to them, enter the house and harm the child.[3]

The y*aloudes* and *stringles* were female monsters that were said to attack pregnant mothers, suck the blood of newborn babies, and kill them.

The *yalou* followed people home after midnight to enter the open door behind them where there were unbaptized children, in order to kill the child. To protect her baby, a mother had to keep a cross made from cane and a piece of bread (on which she had traced the sign of the cross) beneath the child's pillow. Some old women in Apeiranthos, Naxos, told Charles Stewart that they used to read the special *yalou* prayer, so that *xotika* would not get in and strangle their children at night. This prayer contains an exorcism directed at the *yalou,* who was forced to reveal her many names either to SS. Sisfnios and Isidoros or to the Archangel Michael, who would then drive her out of the house.[4]

More widespread was dread of the *Stringles.* These were witch-women with breath of deadly poison, who had the power of changing their form, who flew by night in the shape of crows, sucking human blood.[5] They were generally pictured as tall, skinny women, with long eyebrows and eyes of differing colours. They also had very long finger and toenails, and twisted hands and feet. A woman of Karpathos who lost eight children to the *stringles* said that she heard scratching like the nails of their toes on the floor when they came to suffocate them. She gave birth to her eighth child in someone else's house, and that one was saved.[6] In parts of the Peloponnese it was believed that the island of Mykonos was infested with *stringles*, and mothers would sometimes quieten their naughty children by threatening to call a *stringlas* from Mykonos to take them away.[7] On Karpathos, *stringles* were girls conceived on the night of March 24-5th and born during the Twelve days of Christmas,[8] who, in addition to murdering babies, spent much of their nights in the graveyards digging up dead bodies.[9]

In Arcadia, the *mora* was a hairy, ugly creature, which would attack people. Adults it would strike with dizziness, but newly born babies it would suffocate. The mothers would try to seize her bonnet in order to gain power over it and force it to leave her baby alone. The creature would offer gold florins to get the bonnet back, but the mother must not agree, for they would turn to ashes in her hands.[10]

These creatures recall the *Mormo* and the *Empusas* of ancient times, which were child-killing demons which attended upon the Goddess Hecate. In the ancient world mothers also feared the *strix*, a vampire-witch which took the form of a bird by night and came to suck the blood of infants at night. Its activity was betrayed by general pallor and the marks of the witch's talons on the baby.[11] There is clearly an unbroken tradition with modern folk beliefs here. Cot deaths are still something of a mystery even today, and it would appear that the *yelio* or *stringla* provide a pre-scientific explanation for a baffling phenomenon.

These female child-killing demons were also sometimes portrayed as seductresses, preying on young men as well as children, and extending their range of activities to include adults.

The following story was told in Messenia: Once upon a time, a man was passing the night at the house of a friend, who lived with his wife and mother-in-law. About midnight a noise awakened him, and listening intently he made out the voices of the two women conversing together. What he heard terrified him, for they were planning to eat himself or his host, whichever was the fatter. At once he perceived that his friend's wife and mother-in-law were *stringles*, and knowing that there was no other means of escaping the danger that was threatening him, he determined to try to save himself by guile. The *stringles* approached the supposedly sleeping men in the dark and took hold of their guest's foot to see if it was heavy, and consequently fat and good for eating. He, however, under-standing their purpose, raised his foot of his own accord as they took it in their hands and weighed it, so that it felt to them as light as a feather, and they let it drop again disappointed. Then they took hold of the foot of the other man who was sleeping, and naturally found it heavier. Delighted at the result of their investigation, they ripped open the wretched man's breast, pulled out his liver and other parts, and threw them among the hot ashes on the hearth to cook. Then, noticing that they had no wine, they flew off to the wine-shop, took what they wanted and returned. But in the interval the guest got up, collected the flesh that was being cooked, stowed it away in his pouch, and put in its place on the hearth some animal dung. When they returned, the *stringles* greedily gobbled it up, complaining only that it was somewhat overdone. The next day the two friends rose and left the house. The victim of the previous night was very pale, but he did not bear the slightest wound or scar on his breast. He remarked to his companion that he felt excessively hungry, and the other gave him the meat which had been cooked during the night, which he ate and found very invigorating; the blood mounted to his cheeks and he was soon perfectly sound again. Then his friend told him what had happened, and they returned together and slew the *stringles*.[12]

Unfortunately, in some parts of Greece, when a woman had several children which died, leaving one alive, the survivor was labelled *stringliko*., and held responsible for their deaths. Such a child, it was believed, would not itself live long.[13] A story from Tinos, told of an infant princess who was a *Stringlas*. Every day one of the king's horses was found to have been killed and devoured in the night. The three princes, her brothers, therefore kept watch in turn; and it was the youngest, owing to his courage and skill, who detected the malefactor. About midnight he heard a noise, and fired into the middle of a cloud that seemed to hang over the horses, thereby so wounding his sister that the mark observed on her next day betrayed her nightly doings. Not daring however to accuse her to his father, he fled from home with his mother to a place of safety, while the girl remained undisturbed in her voracity and consumed one by one all the people of the town.[14]

Some creatures were intimately associated with sleep disturbances of various kinds.

In Mani sleepwalkers were known as *stringloparmeni*, or "witch-taken ones." The witches were believed to be trying to lure them into the hills under their bewitchment, where they would be horribly tortured.[15]

In Macedonia it was one's own shadow which did this.[16] However, problems of sleep were more usually associated with the *Sphragnas* and the *Moros*.

On Samos, the *sphragnas* was said to resemble a small boy in a glittering, sequined golden bonnet. Its habit was to enter a house and sit on the chests of sleeping people, preventing them from breathing properly, and so suffocating them. A way of avoiding its attentions was to take a piece of bread into the toilet, and offer it to the *sphragnas* while thus engaged. The surprisingly fastidious creature would be so disgusted by this behaviour that it would not afterwards even approach the person.[17]

More usually it was the *mora*, a species of male *lamia*, who roamed abroad by night. If he espied a sleeper by the road, he would sit upon his chest and grow so heavy that the sleeper would bellow like a bull. But if by chance the victim were not quite fast asleep, and seeing him approach could stealthily snatch his cap, he would fall into his power, and would grant him all he wished.[18] In Athens, the *moros* resembled a small black dog, which searched for sleepers and troubled them by sitting on them, producing a weight on their stomachs and bad dreams. Sometimes the sleepers would moan and groan, and would not be able to wake up.[19]

During recent centuries the urban populations living on the shores of the Mediterranean Sea have been repeatedly plagued by various epidemic diseases, such as smallpox, cholera, typhoid, and others, which frequently caused great mortality. Their cause was not understood, and magic was used to try to evade their devastating effects.

The inhabitants of Prosymna, in the Argolid, at the end of the nineteenth century, threatened with plague which was ravaging neighbouring villages, tried to hold up its spread by hammering three large nails into a rock and praying that they would "hold" the disease. They did avoid infection, and put their deliverance down to their preventive measures.[20]

Attempts were sometimes made to create a barrier around the village, which the disease would not be able to penetrate. When the French fleet brought cholera to Athens, following an ancient practice, all the girls of Maroussi met together in a single house in the town and spun a long ribbon in one day with which to encircle the entire village. Sometimes the efforts to create a "zone of safety" were much more elaborate.

"The bubonic plague could not come to Panorio because the people had drawn a circle around the village using a plough pulled by twin calves. They chose calves because calves licked Christ when he was born and consequently calves are on good terms with Christianity. They buried those calves alive after they ploughed that circle and [the plague] didn't come here."[21]

The following took place in Thrace: "Kastanies was hemmed by seven tall trees . . . They were old, ancient; the one far from the other . . . If they heard of disease in the neighbouring villages, they would hold an all night service so that it would not enter Kastanies. The next morning they would read the liturgy. Afterwards, they brought out the large icons from the church, the *sikhna,* and chanting, they made a circuit around the outskirts of the village. While making this circuit they would stop at each tree, and the priest would carve out a round piece from the body of the tree using a small knife. He would then affix this to the tree a little bit higher up using wax. Then they would proceed back to the church where the people would disperse. In this fashion the village would close shut, by the grace and strength of God, as well as by their own faith. The disease would not go [to them]."[22]

Single standing columns of marble were sometimes considered to hold diseases, so that removing them would release an epidemic. During the period of Turkish rule, in the popular mind ancient columns, when they survived singly, came to be thought of as imprisoning curses. Most of these curses were thought to be epidemic diseases of various kinds.

The fate of a single broken column near the present Piraeus Street was once believed to be connected with the health of the city of Athens, in that if it fell, an epidemic would break out, since the disease was believed to be trapped underneath it. The column was said to have been erected by forty women who had collected money to buy a cart, to which they yoked calves. They also purchased a silver vessel, wrote down the names of the various epidemic diseases to which the population was liable, enclosed them inside the vessel, and then it, the cart and the calves were buried, and the column placed on top of them in honour of Saint Haralambos, protector against plagues. This column was removed, fortunately without triggering an outbreak of disease, in 1835; but a similar column remains standing today in the district of Metaxurgeio, protected by a church.[23]

Most infectious diseases are grammatically feminine in the Greek language, and the Greeks used to personify them as old women. Some saw the Plague as an old black-clad woman who went from house to house after dark. Others imagined her as a blind woman who had to keep to the walls to get about. To protect oneself from infection it was necessary to sit and sleep in the middle of the room.

During the nineteenth century the story was told of a coach driver who claimed that at about midnight one night near the church of Saint Mavros in Athinas Street, in Athens, he picked up a woman dressed in black who asked to be taken to the Monument of Lysikrates in the Plaka. When they arrived at their destination he turned around, only to find, to his amazement, not one but three women, all similarly dressed, and all getting out of the carriage together. None of them turned around to pay the fare as they got out, but so surprised was he that he just sat there and watched them walk way. On the next day, he heard that the cholera had broken out in that neighbourhood.

On another occasion, an old woman encountered two mysterious women who were strangers to her, dressed entirely in white, at the cave below the Observatory, on the Hill of the Nymphs. Curious, she watched to see which road they would take. Soon afterwards, an epidemic of smallpox broke out in the area towards which they had travelled. For the people of the time, the implication was clear.[24]

The terrible scourge of smallpox was personified in Macedonia as a female *xotika*, often designated by various flattering epithets, such as the "Gracious " or " Pitiful" and *Vloya,* a name which is by some considered a euphemistic term which may mean a "Blessing" or an inflammation. The term "Lady Small-Pox" is applied to the disease. When someone was ill with the disease she was propitiated in the following manner: A stool or a small table, covered with a snow-white cloth, was placed beside the bed in which the patient lay. Upon it were laid two or three buns and bouquets of flowers, adorned with gold leaf. The room was kept scrupulously clean and, tidy, so that the "Lady" may not be offended. No spinning, knitting, weaving, or other "woman's labour," was allowed in the dwelling throughout the " Lady's" stay, for it was believed that she liked to repose upon the wool and cotton. For a similar reason, there was no washing of clothes with hot water, lest the steam should disturb the goddess. Honey was sprinkled over the walls in various parts of the house, and especially in the sickroom, that the goddess might taste it, and her temper assimilate some of its sweetness. Sugar-plums were scattered over the stairs. Instrumental music was played. These efforts at rendering the goddess sweet-tempered were reinforced by traditional wish of visitors: "May she be sweet as honey."[25]

The logical consequences of such a superstition are evident in a story from Palaiotsiveri, in the Argolid, where many people once died of plague. An old man in the village decided that a particular silent and unapproachable old woman was the plague. With the help of two other men, he strangled her. From that moment the plague went away, and even those who were already ill recovered. The survivors, who moved to found the present village of Tsiveri, considered that his actions had delivered them from death.[26]

In some places, e.g. Andros and Kythera, consumption was attributed to demons, called "Furies" (Erinyes), eating up the vital organs of the diseased person. When the sick person died, it was feared that they might seek another body, so young people were kept out of the room, and a hole opened above the head of the corpse for the demons to leave by.[27]

Epidemic diseases which affected the flocks also threatened their keepers' livelihoods, and were much feared.

The nomadic Sarakatsans particularly feared the "Ntaoutes", demons who played the *syrinx*, or shepherd's pipes. This powerful satyr-shaped demon with cloven hoofs and rams' horns, was liable to play tricks on the animals, and had the ability to instil them with panic. These creatures were particularly dangerous to the flocks just before and during the lambing season, just before leaving for the summer pastures and in the height of summer. They would swoop shrieking on the flocks like birds of prey. Afterwards, the animals would swell up and die.[28]

In the Pindus they would seek to kill the spirit by firing guns into the air.[29] The chief remedy, however, was to leave the fold immediately and in darkness. The flock had to be separated from the dogs, since the *Ntaoutes* had the knack of making friends with them.[30] The bells of the animals were removed, and the move was made in silence, so that the *Ntaoutes* would not follow. The Sarakatsans would also lead the flock through a village, hoping that the spirit would stay in the village. This was another reason for removing the bells from the animals, so that they would not wake the villagers, who would kill the animals if they found out that they were being moved at night. They would guess the reason for the move, and believing that the Ntaoutes or other malign creatures would probably be following, and could attack the cattle and other animals of the villages, would take no risks. The infected flock might first be taken to a chapel of Profitis Ilias, where it would be led in a circle around the chapel three times, before being blessed, and then moved on to a new site. The new fold would be blessed with holy water by a priest, the animals' bells would also be blessed before being returned to them, and the new fold would be surrounded with a ring of smoke. Old shoes, hair and the hides of slaughtered animals would be burned to create a stench which, it was said, snakes and wolves would flee.[31] If they were not able to leave the place where they were, they had to get three priests to bring the holy mysteries (the bread and wine of the Communion) to the place and carry them three times around the boundaries of the pasture, each one erecting a wooden cross.[32] In addition to the *Ntaoutes*, there were the Shadowy Ones and the *Kalotches* who also preyed upon their beasts.[33]

In Macedonia a Mohammedan dervish would be hired to exorcise a herd of cattle. He would draw a circle around the flock while chanting a spell. Then he would take a passage from the Koran wrapped in a leather pouch and throw it into the herd. The animal which it struck would be the one harbouring the evil spirit. A flock of sheep would also be circumscribed, in this case, but the charm would be suspended from the leader of the flock.[34]

Abbott had the good fortune to witness himself the exorcism cattle after an outbreak of disease at Nigrita in southern Macedonia. "The cattle of the district had been attacked by a disease which was, as a matter of course, set down to the agency of the Evil One. The people, therefore, resolved to have it exorcised. On a Saturday evening the town-crier proclaimed that the cattle affected should be driven next morning to the enclosure of the church. On the morrow many head of cattle of all ages and complexions, and of both sexes, congregated in the church-yard, awaiting the special ceremony, which was to be performed for their benefit. When the ordinary Sunday service was over, the priest came out with the hand of Saint Dionysios, the patron saint of the village, carried before him. He then read the customary prayer, commending each particular ox, cow, and calf by name to the mercy of Heaven. At the mention of the bovine names-such as Black, Red, Dapple, Moraite, etc., the officiator was so strongly moved by the humour of the situation that he could hardly refrain from bursting into laughter - an emotion in which some of the farmers themselves were not disinclined to join. But, though far from blind to the ludicrous side of the affair, they were too much in earnest about their cattle to interrupt the rite"[35]

The name *Ntaoutis* was given to a spirit which lived in a *katavothra* on Mount Oitia and roamed the mountainsides. It was described as having a form similar to a large black mouse with prominent ears, which walked on two feet. It sucked the milk of sheep and goats. Shortly afterwards, the animals would die.[36]

The *Ntaoutes* was perhaps identical with the dreaded *smerdaki* or *hamadryad*. This would usually appear in the form of a billy-goat or a ram among the flock when grazing in the pastures, and cause them to panic. It would mount the animals, which would soon fall sick. Their bellies would swell up, and their flesh, and even their blood, blacken, and they would die very quickly. The meat of animals killed by the *smerdaki* was itself regarded as dangerous to eat. This creature could also appear as a small hairy boy[37] or a hairy kitten with the cry of a child.[38]

In Messenia they compared the *smerdaki* to a greyhound that hunted sheep and especially goats. When it mounted them, they would die on the next day. Their meat looked bruised, and the dogs would not touch it. Sometimes, in the middle of the night, when everyone was sleeping, the animals would become panicked because the greyhound was hunting them. Here, as in the north, it was customary for the shepherd to get three priests in vestments with the bread and wine of the Communion to go to the fold singing psalms of blessing, and for each to erect a wooden cross. Then the *smerdaki* would cease bothering the sheep.[39]

Clearly, the *Ntaoutes* and *smerdaki* were none other than the goat-shaped, panic-inducing, ancient god Pan.[40] Even now, the islanders of Zakynthos know him as Panos or Panios, where he haunts caves[41] and ravines.[42]

There were, however, other folk explanations of those demons. It was often believed that infants who died unbaptized became *smerdakia,* and so threatened the animals.[43] In Stemnitsa, in Arcadia, next to the church of Zoodocho Pigis, is a small graveyard for such children. Many claimed to have seen small children at midnight above the wall of the cemetery.[44]

Rarely, nereids could prove dangerous to the flocks. Nympholepsy could also affect animals as much as humans. A shepherd of Skopelos told Lawson of a wild goat which he had tamed, and which mixed with his herd, took to haunting the immediate neighbourhood of a nereid-haunted cave on a bare and rocky hillside, and in consequence grew thin from want of food.[45] The number of chapels on Folegandros was explained by the desire to have protecting saints near the flocks to prevent this.[46]

Three nereids were supposed to have invaded the village of Stimangas, in Korinthia in the form of a small dog, where they caused many animals to die. The villagers ploughed up the soil at intervals around the village, and buried bottles of holy water, which solved the problem.[47]

The Macedonians believed in the existence of vampires which exclusively preyed upon cattle and sheep, riding on their shoulders and sucking their blood. Professional "vampire exterminators" would hire themselves out to get rid of them. These were usually Mohammedan dervishes, who would carry an iron spit with an iron spit with a sharp point as a sign of their vocation.[48] On Samos these vampires would suck the milk of the goats at night. People caught one by ambushing it and shooting it. They cut him into four pieces, and found the tell-tale milk in his intestines.[49]

Xotika were not merely dangerous to cattle as agents of disease. They could kill in other ways. One time when a flock was taken into the Pindus to graze over the summer, the shepherd watered it at a particular trough near a hole. Suddenly a black and golden ram appeared and went through the panic-stricken flock mounting the ewes, before disappearing. When, in January, those ewes gave birth, the lambs were all so well-formed and beautiful that it was decided not to put any under the knife, but to allow them to breed. When the flock was taken up into the mountains for the next summer, and arrived once again at the spot where the black and golden lamb had first appeared, it returned and the lambs all followed it, and were lost. From that time on, shepherds have avoided that trough and hole as haunted.

The following story, told by a Macedonian shepherd, attributed disaster to a flock in a similar manner. The shepherd was with the flock in the Xerovounia in the 1860s, at a lake reputed to be haunted. For that reason they only watered sheep there, never goats, horses or other large animals. During the night a sheep appeared which was white all over with black spots only on its head. It emerged from the lake, and promptly mounted seventy-two sheep. These bore seventy-two lambs, all completely black, even though the ram was mostly white. Some time later, when the flock went down to drink, the strange ram emerged once more from the waters. The lambs which it had sired went into the lake with it and disappeared. The shepherd was able to save only two.[50]

Stringlos was a creature which preyed on both men and animals. It could be heard in lonely places as "a voice, something of air, which appears in the darkness and wilderness. Sometimes you hear him coming as the galloping of a horse. Yet a few moments later he will be heard in the far distance. If you say a prayer, the Lord's Prayer, or the Apostles Creed, he will disappear ... There are two places where it is to be heard. One of them is a deep gorge right outside the village, the other is on the mountain- side where they take the goats to feed."[51]

It was described as having a thick, wild hoarse voice, which is heard now here, and a moment later perhaps two kilometres away. Researchers were told: "We are country people and we know the animals and the birds, but *Stringlos* resembles none of these - he is air, he is shadow."[52]

His voice was frequently heard when someone in the village was going to die. The very voice could itself cause death. "It cries and tries to frighten you; one can get a heart attack from that." However, some held that it did no harm unless you are so frightened that you died from fear itself.[53]

Another man saw *Stringlos* on the road in the form of a baby. He picked it up to carry along, but fortunately he soon understood what it was, for it got heavier and heavier. When he realized what it was he threw it as far as he could. The stringlos shouted then, "Oh, if only you had held me for a few minutes more!"[54]

Another testified: "I have heard a story of *Stringlos* which I believe, for the man who told me is a very serious and honest man. An army major, along with several men, one of whom was my friend, went rabbit hunting at night out in the wild country towards the old acropolis. They were in the army jeep and it was about midnight. Suddenly in front of the head-lights they saw about twenty yards ahead of them a half man, that is the top half of a man, the bottom, shaggy like a furry animal, but hard to see, dancing and prancing. He kept dancing along in front of the car. It was *Stringlos* of course. The major levelled his rifle to shoot but was so afraid he couldn't hold the weapon. They turned the jeep around and drove back to Doxario as fast as they could. My friend was so frightened he went to bed and slept for twenty-four hours. When he told the story to me he was so upset that he cried."[55]

The main problem with *Stringlos* was that he was thought to suck the milk of the sheep, or have intercourse with them, causing them to die. Shepherds would change the bells on the animals, putting sheep bells on the goats and vice versa, so that he would be confused and the animals saved.[56]

"As a small girl I took the sheep to graze. One night as some sheep were lagging behind I made them jump to the whip and as I was doing that I heard a sound as though a puppy were whining - although there was no dog or puppy among the animals. On the following morning, as we were milking the sheep we heard the same whining voice and found some more dead animals. We realized it was Stringlos who, disguised as a puppy and then as a calf, had killed the animals. We knew that if you try to kill the animal into which you think he is disguised losses will come to you, so we called the priest who read the special prayer, and no more deaths occurred.[57] Protection against Stringlos included charms made out of incense or the pages of church service books and the herb rue.[58]

A tradition said that he was the son of a very beautiful young woman who was found dead at the seashore by a man. When he found her the man raped her. The child born from that act was *Stringlos*: antichristian and the embodiment of evil.[59]

---

[1] McNall 70.

[2] Stewart 100.

[3] Stewart 100.

[4] Stewart 101-2.

[5] Rodd 187.

[6] Νουάρου 246.

[7] Πολίτης 1:371.

[8] Νουάρου 237.

[9] Νουάρου 246.

[10] Πολίτες 1:406-7.

[11] Halliday 53.

[12] Lawson 182-3.

[13] Κωστάκης 75.

[14] Lawson 183.

[15] e.g. Fermor (2) 68.

[16] Abbott 257.

[17] Πολίτες 1:406.

[18] Πολίτη 1:406.

[19] Βούρνας & Γαρίδη 184.

[20] Σεραφείμ 354.

[21] Blum & Blum 104-5.

[22] Κυριακίδου-Νέστορος.

[23] See Tomkinson (1) 108-9.

[24] Tomkinson (1) 108-9.

[25] Abbott 236-7.

[26] Τσικλίδες (2) 1:226.

[27] Bent 211.

[28] Fermor (2) 38.

[29] Παπακωνσταντίνου 350.

[30] Fermor (2) 38.

[31] Παπακωνσταντίνου 350.

[32] Πολίτης 1:316.

[33] Fermor (2) 38.

[34] Abbott 224.

[35] Abbott 223-4.

[36] Γιαννουλακης (1) 299.

[37] Γιαννουλακης (1) 299.

[38] Κωστάκης 81.

[39] Πολίτη 1. 231.

[40] Γιαννουλάκης (1) 300.

[41] Παπακωνσταντίνου 350.

[42] Πολίτης 1:230

[43] Κωστάκης 79.

[44] Τσικλίδης (2) 2:195.

[45] Lawson 135.

[46] Fermor (1) 170.

[47] Τσικλίδης (2) 2.

[48] Abbott 221.

[49] Blum & Blum 75-76.

[50] Πολίτης 1:230.

[51] Blum & Blum 96.

[52] Blum & Blum 96.

[53] Blum & Blum 97.

[54] Blum & Blum 97.

[55] Blum & Blum 97.

[56] Blum & Blum 97.

[57] Blum & Blum 97.

[58] Blum & Blum 97.

[59] Blum & Blum 96.

Death, and the Walking Dead

Death in modem Greece still retains distinctly pagan associations. Hades is the destination of the dead, while Charos is their ever-watchful guardian. Punishment for sin takes place in the fiery river of Tartarus. Christianity has adapted rather than replaced the ancient cosmology and myths. The archangel Michael functions as the modem Hermes. It used to be believed that on November 8, the feast of Saint Michael in the Orthodox Church, he goes over the list drawn up by the Fates and writes down the names of those who will die during the ensuing year.

Charon, the boatman who ferried the dead across the River Styx in ancient mythology, is well known in Greece today as Charos. Although he has come to personify death itself, he is not the familiar Western skeleton with a scythe in his hand. Instead, a dark man of huge stature and flaming fiery eyes, he travels around on horseback to collect the dead when their time is up, sometimes lurking in ambush to surprise his victims. Noises and convulsions made by the dying are interpreted as his struggle with Charos, who has arrived to take him away.[1] This is so

vividly imagined that people who believe themselves to be dying sometimes "see" him standing before them. For example, a young girl called
out, just before her death: "There he is! A young man is coming with a
spear to cut me up! Bring me the long knife. He is going to slaughter
me."[2]

Charos was not without sympathy for those whose lives were cut
short by the inexorable decrees of God or the Fates, and his occasional
unwillingness to execute their harsh commands is illustrated in
numerous folk-songs; particularly when some brave youth, a shepherd
or warrior, aroused his compassion. One story related to John Lawson,
shows him as a friend of man.

Once upon a time, a man and his wife had seven children, all of whom
died in infancy. When an eighth was born, the father went to a witch and
enquired how he might best ensure the boy's life. She told him that the
others had died because he had chosen unsuitable godparents, and
instructed him on this occasion to ask the first man whom he should meet
on his way home to stand sponsor for the child. He set out for home, and
almost immediately encountered an imposing stranger riding on a black
horse, and made his request to him. The stranger consented, and the
baptism at once took place; but no sooner was it over than the stranger
disappeared, without so much as telling his name.

Ten years passed, and the child grew strong and healthy. Then at last
the father again encountered the unknown stranger, and reproached him
with having been absent so long without ever making any enquiries
about his godson. The stranger answered, "Better for you if I had not
come now, and if you did not need to learn my name. I am Charos, and
because I am your friend I have come to warn you that your days are well-
nigh over." Thereupon Charos led him to a cave in the mountainside,
which they entered, and came to a chamber where were many candles
burning. Then Charos said, " Look! Those candles are the lives of men,
and over there are yours and your son's." Then the man looked, and saw
that his son's was tall and burnt slowly, but that there were only a couple
of inches left of his own candle. He asked Charos to light yet another
candle for him before his own was burnt away; but Charos answered that
that could not be. Then he pleaded with him to give him ten years from
the life of his son, for he was a poor man, and if he died before his son
were grown to manhood, his widow and orphan would be in want. But
Charos answered: "In no way can the decreed length of life be changed.
Yet will I show you how, in the two years that yet remain to you, you may
enrich yourself, and leave abundant store for your wife and child. You

shall become a physician. It does not matter that you know nothing of medicine, for I will give you knowledge better than that of drugs. Your eyes will always be open to see me. When you go to a sick man's bed, if you see me standing at the head, you will know then that he must die, and you will say to those who summoned you that no skill could save him. But if you see me standing at the foot of the bed, then you will know that he will recover. In that case, give him pills made out of bread, or something like that, and promise to restore him." The man thanked Charos, and went home.

Now it chanced that at that time, the only daughter of the king lay seriously ill, and all the doctors and magicians had been called to heal her, but they could do nothing. Then the poor man whom Charos had taught went into the room where the princess lay, and saw Charos, but he was standing at the foot of her bed. So he told the king to send away the other physicians, for he alone could heal her. He went home and mixed flour and water and returned and gave it to the king's daughter, and she soon recovered. Then the king gave him a great present, and he became famous, so that many resorted to him, and soon he was rich. In this way, the two years passed, and at the end of it, he himself lay sick. When he saw Charos standing at the head of his bed, he told his wife turn the bed around, but it did not work, for Charos again stood at his head. As he opened his mouth to cry out, Charos caught him by the hair and took his soul.[3]

Despite the apparent impossibility of evading Charos, it was the custom that the mothers of Mani, if they had lost their firstborn male child in infancy would attempt to deceive him by a crude ruse. They would take their second baby out into the street, held in their aprons, shouting, "A lamb for sale. Who will buy a lamb?" The first passer-by would say, "I will." He would hand over a small sum of money, and act as godfather for him at the baptism. Then he would return him to his mother.[4]

In an interesting parallel with the relationship, in traditional Christianity, between Christ and his mother, during the nineteenth century, many people on Naxos believed that intercession with Charos' mother might cause him to stay his hand for a while.[5]

It was widely believed in Greece that after death the spirit separated from the body and wandered the neighbourhood for three nights in the form of a cloud or ball: white if the person was good, and black if evil. In the room where a person has died, a light might be kept burning, and the shutters left open, so that the spirit could come and go as it pleased. In many places, the soul was thought to wander for forty days, visiting the places it had loved during its lifetime. For that reason, the dead would return to people in dreams and visions during those days.[6] On Karpathos, the spirit of a dead person was likened to a bird; and if a bird entered a house, people would say that it was a dead soul revisiting its old haunts.[7] In the Mani, region a man was thought to become a werewolf for forty days, and range about his old haunts. All missing food was attributed to such werewolf haunting.[8]

Haunting by ghosts was considered a frequent occurrence, because some spirits continue to haunt the earth beyond the allotted period. Thus a villager in Attica related: "My brother was coming back from the mines late one evening and decided to take a short-cut through the woods that led by the stream. As he rounded a turn in the path, he saw a ghost sitting on a rock. The ghost looked like a priest to him. Not stopping to look back, he turned and ran back the way he had come and arrived home exhausted an hour later. Our family was convinced that he had seen the ghost of a dead priest, or the Devil disguised as a priest. We knew that he saw it, too, for Yanni is neither stupid or crazy."[9]

Such ghosts were generally supposed to be those of animals or people whose blood had been shed in that place; or people who had died unburied, and unblessed by the rites of the Church.[10] In the Mani, where violent crime called for vengeance, a man's blood was said to shout aloud on the day he died, and blood shed by violence would remain wet until a wooden cross had been driven into the ground on the spot.[11]

Thus accidental or violent death was thought to be responsible for many hauntings. One day, two boys went to hunt birds on a rock in the river in Kastri, near Kynouria, in Arcadia. One of them slipped, fell into the river and drowned. After that his voice was often heard calling people to go down to the river. Many went, but none ever saw anything.[12] The ghost of a priest haunts a cave at the foot of the rocks of Kokkina, near Ahladokampo, in the Argolid, where many years ago, (it is not known how long ago), a priest fell to his death while gathering wild honey.[13]

Typical of a haunting caused by violent death is the following story from the village of Apano Loutro, in Korinthia. A girl named Chrysoula used to graze her father's animals in a ravine near the village. She was loved by a young man of the village, who sought her hand in marriage. But since his family had connections with the Turks, and were considered traitors, his father would not consent to it. In bitter revenge, one day when Chryssoula went down to the ravine to drink, the young man came upon her from behind with a scimitar and cut off her head. It rolled onto a rock still called today Chryssoula's rock. From that moment, until her family took revenge for her murder, she would appear in the ravine as a small white puppy. The village avenged her death by hanging the young man's head from an olive tree, which thereupon became barren. Yet even today, animals which are led down into the ravine of Chryssoula flee from the place with their tails in the air.[14]

Greece's often violent past means that many places are haunted by unquiet spirits for the same reason. For example, the site of the archaeological excavations at Akrotiri, on Santorini, is said to be haunted. Shortly after the digging began local people began to complain that they could not work in the fields because of the ghosts. One testified: "One morning when I went to collect the tomatoes and it was not yet sunrise, a big white light covered a great ghost, covered with a shield. There were many, all in movement, yet they looked firm. They went toward the sea in the direction opposite from the sunrise to escape from the light which goes towards the west."[15]

A figure clad in the *foustanella*, or kilt, the standard dress of the male in many parts of Greece until nineteenth century, features in many tales of this kind. For example, at the time of the War of Independence, an important chief shepherd (or *tselingas)* was found dead at the sink-hole (*katavothra*) of Vlachernas, near Chotousas in Arcadia. It was not clear whether it was an accident or suicide. Afterwards the shepherds of the neighbourhood saw him in the night each summer. They were not afraid of him, and considered that spotting him would bring them good luck. Then one morning in 1933 another man was found drowned in the same place. He also was also seen afterwards haunting the area.[16]

It is not always clear, however, whether such an apparition is a ghost or *xotikò*. The area known as Portes, on Mount Lyrkeion, in the Argolid, is haunted by a large man clad in a foustanella, who appears in the middle of the day and throws rocks at people. But it is not clear if he is a ghost or a spirit of that place.[17]

Sometimes it is guilt which keeps a soul wandering abroad. At the time of the War of Independence, a great tree in the district of Glyka Nera, on the central plain of Attica, was used by a Moor who acted as executioner for the Turks, hanging his victims from its branches or slaughtering them at its foot. Many freedom fighters were executed in this way, both before and during the war. When the Turks fled, they left their executioner behind. At first some passers-by tried to kill him. When one, named Kosta, caught hold of him in order to strangle him like a kid, for he had killed his father and grandfather, he heard the voice of his forebears telling him to desist, since the Moor was not responsible for what he had done. Later someone else, probably the son of another one of his victims, did kill him. Afterwards, the Moor's tree had the reputation of being haunted. It was said that the executioner would emerge from a great hollow inside and accost passers-by, weeping and beating his breast, and crying that he was not guilty of the crimes he had committed, since they had been forced on him by the Turks. He would plead with them to exorcise him with priestly rites and forgiveness. When he saw that they were not inclined to do this, he would resort to threatening them, and blaspheming and cursing.[18]

On occasion, a benign ghost has been "adopted" by its community, almost as a mascot. Haimana, the famous ghost of Amphissa, has become almost a "town spirit." On Saturday nights, it was said to walk the alleys of the district where the tanners used to work, starting from the brook of Kolokythou. A very traditional, "gothic" spectre, it was inclined to moan and rattle its chains. Today there is an impressive torchlight procession during the annual carnival celebrations which commemorates his walk.[19]

Ghosts, or revenants, in Greece tend to be seen out of doors, unlike their more housebound northern neighbours. Yet despite this preference, Greece was not without its haunted houses. A "haunted house" was one inhabited by an evil or troublesome spirit, rather than a "regular", benign house spirit. Its presence and its malignity was usually most evidently manifest in the consistent ill-fortune of those who lived in it. These malevolent spirits might disturb the peace of the household by making mysterious noises, by throwing bricks and stones, by sitting on sleepers' chests in the form of a hideous nightmare or shadow, and by teasing and worrying the inmates of the house at unreasonable hours.

Malevolent spirits could only be expelled by a religious ceremony of exorcism. The priest would read a special service, bless the house using holy water sprinkled with a bunch of basil, and charge all evil and unclean spirits to depart from it forthwith. But it sometimes happened that the ghosts defied his prayers, and, in spite of holy water and exorcisms, they persisted in vexing the inhabitants. In that case, the house was deserted and shunned.[20] Bent found several such abandoned houses on Kimolos when he visited that island.[21]

The newspaper *Kairoi* reported such an "unlucky" house in Kyparissia, in Messene, in 1893. The house of the inheritance of Tourkolia had no sooner been built, than within a few months the woman of the house fell ill and died. Her husband died eight days later. Then their children died, one by one. After that, everyone else fled the unlucky building. It was then leased to a tenant, who lost his eldest son, and left the house before the expiry of the lease. The next tenant was a pharmacist named Despototopoulos. His only son, a twelve year-old boy, committed suicide after inadvertently shooting another boy. After that, the house remained deserted.

Number 261, Vasilissis Olgas, in Thessaloniki, opposite the County Hall (*nomarchia*), earned for itself an unenviable reputation. Originally a Jewish casino, built in 1918, it is now used as a store for household goods. No one knows why the building seemed to be cursed, but after the Second World War, all the contractors who undertook to demolish it suffered unpleasant consequences. The more fortunate merely suffered various strokes of bad luck, while the less fortunate died prematurely. Three who were to be involved in its demolition died on the very night that work started. The contractor died of a heart attack in Thessaloniki, while the engineer and architect were killed in a road accident on the road from Athens. It is reported that refugees from Asia Minor who took shelter in the building during the early 1920s were frequently terrified by sudden loud and alarming noises, which they compared to the nearby passage of a railway train. After they left, a gipsy family moved in. They literally ran away on their first evening in the house. A researcher has identified this building as one which was occupied during the last years of Ottoman rule by a Turkish bey who was said to have murdered his wives.[22]

A house in the district of Dimitroulia, New Corinth, was said to be haunted. People who spent the night there claim to have seen two women dressed in white, followed by a large goose. Strange sounds, such as banging of the furniture also disturbed the rest of the place. Conditions got so bad that it is now uninhabited. It is said that its foundations disturbed the remains of an older building, possible a ruined church.[23]

In the second part of the twentieth century, many hauntings were associated with the cruelties of the Second World War. The screams of tortured victims of the Nazi occupiers could still be heard at night, many years later, coming from some of the buildings in which they originally suffered.

Until very recently, on the borders of Pikermi and Pallene, in the central plain of Attica, stood the ruins of a very strange house, which had the reputation of being haunted by moving lights and the sounds of groaning and dragging chains. It was said that birds would not alight on it, or fly over it. It was built at the beginning of the twentieth century by Pericles Kallergi, estate manager of the wealthy Skouze family. It possessed several curious design features which are very difficult to account for in an ordinary dwelling-house. It stood quite alone in an open field, lacking any kind of yard or garden. It was not possible to move from the lower floor to the bedroom on the upper floor inside the building; it was necessary first to go outside onto the roof. The cellars were similarly inaccessible from inside the building. The interior decoration of the rooms was unorthodox, and unusually lurid. All these things raised in many peoples' minds the question as to what the house was originally designed for. Kallergi himself could offer no help. After first murdering his wife, he committed suicide. Then during the Occupation, the house was used as a command post by the Italians, who employed its cellars as a torture chamber. Since that time, the strange phenomena began. Neighbours claimed that they could hear strange noises coming across the fields from the building during the night. One tenant fled the premises after staying there for only a short time. As a consequence, it became impossible to let the house. Enthusiasts for the paranormal have claimed that strange impressions appeared on photographs taken there, together with other unusual phenomena.[24]

Few countries have such an eventful a past as Greece, site of so many of the most famous battles of history: Marathon, Thermopylai, Salamis, Plataea, Navarino, Messolonghi. The names roll off the tongue like a roll call of military honours. Pausanius recorded that in his time, the battle-field of Marathon was believed to be haunted by the ghosts of the slain. In the nineteenth century, sixteen hundred years after Pausanias, and over two thousand years after the battle, the same tradition was still alive in Vrana: that the whinnying of horses, the sounds of battle and the voices of people in torment could sometimes be heard during the night across the plain. When anyone approached the area from which the sounds seemed to come, they would recede into the distance or be silenced.[25]

Perhaps the most famous haunted battlefield in Greece today is the site of a comparatively minor incident in the recent struggle of the Greeks of the island of Crete for their independence. In May 1828, the Cretans at Frangocastello revolted against Turkish rule. The local chiefs decided to abandon the castle and retreat into the mountains, where they could fight a guerrilla war. One rebel leader, however, the Epirote, Hadjimichaelis Dalianis, refused to abandon the stronghold, and stubbornly remained with his force inside the walls. These men were besieged by the Turks for seven days before the defenders were slaughtered. Dalliani was beheaded, and his head sent to the Pasha. Since that time, it is said that every year, in the early morning mists a little before dawn on May 28th, a column of armed infantry and cavalry dressed in black may be seen moving from the direction of the now derelict church of Ayios Haralambos towards Frangocastello. Because of the time of day when they appear, they are called *drossoulites* or "dew-Shades".

Many have tried to explain this phenomenon. Some have said that it is a mirage on the wide plain. But mirages usually occur when the temperature is hot, in the middle of the day. Others have tried to explain the apparition as somehow created by the reflected images of soldiers engaged in military manoeuvres in Libya. But it is highly unlikely that the Libyan army would arrange to hold its manoeuvres each year on the anniversary of this small engagement in Crete; yet it is only at this time of the year that the phenomenon occurs.[26]

Undoubtedly, one of the most feared of the paranormal denizens of Greece was the *vrykolakas*, or vampire. Charles Edwards had this to say about the hardy Cretans he met during the 1880s: "A muscular Cretan, who would not delay to tackle three or four Turks if it were required of him, would be ready to die of dread of a vampire if he saw an inexplicable shadow in the night, and would be for digging up this or that corpse in the neighbouring churchyard, to see if the flush of blood in its normally pale face indicated it as his unholy assailant in the quiet hours."[27]

Few cultures in the world have a tradition of belief in vampires as long-standing and as widespread as Greece. But to understand the character of the Greek vampire, we must divest ourselves of many of the now fashionable associations of the term, derived from the romantic writers of the nineteenth century.

An informant in the USA explained the Greek concept of a vampire to Dorothy Lee thus: "In the homeland they say that a man is a *vrykolakas* when, after three years, they dig up his corpse whole. When the body has melted away, and only bones are left, the relatives go and take the bones, they put them in a little box, they pour wine over them, the priest reads over them, they put them in the *coemeterion* [house of sleep], they put on the box the name of the dead, and the date. But some bodies do not melt away, and of these they say, "He has become a *vrykolakas*." In those years we said that these had been cursed by their father, or that the priest had excommunicated them because they had married a relative; or if they had committed a crime, then they said that this man will come out whole after he dies. Now I don't believe these things, but then I did.

And some people come out of the soil in three years, with flesh on, black and half-decayed. And I saw one, and how could I sleep after that? . . . they had him in the yard of the church, as an example to the people. And after three days his relatives took him, and they had to recite many prayers, and bury him, and again after three years to take him out. Of this they would say that it is a *vrykolakas*, and we would be afraid . . . Such a thing would give rise to gossip and speculation about the man's life."[28]

The normal process of interment in Greece is to bury a body for three years, exhume the bones, and place them in a box in an ossuary. A problem arises, however, when the body has not properly decayed. Today it would be reburied for a further period of three years, but a bishop must exorcise it first.[29] In his *The Greek Islands*, Lawrence Durrell tells of such an exhumation and reburial which had taken place a week before he had arrived in a village. The body had been found fresh with an orange in its hand, which was also still fresh. An otherwise particularly bright boy had taken the orange, and peeled and eaten it. When Durrell arrived, he was a hopeless idiot.[30]

Many reasons are given why a person might become a vampire. He might have died alone, with no one to take care of him. Some animal, especially a cat, might have jumped over his corpse.[31] For some, any living thing, animal, bird, insect or even a candle, should not be allowed to fly, jump or be carried over a corpse for this reason.[32] In Macedonia, a corpse over which a cat had jumped was immediately pierced by two large needles to prevent its becoming a vampire.[33]

Those who had eaten the flesh of a sheep which had been killed by a wolf were in some places said to become vampires. A Cretan belief was that this fate befell those at whose baptism some portion of the ceremony had been read incorrectly or left incomplete. For others, it was those who did not receive the full and due rites of burial. Children conceived on an important religious festival were also liable to become vampires, as well as those who had received a parent's curse.

On Kimolos, Theodore Bent noted that those who had been cursed at the moment of death suffered this fate. Certainly many appropriate curses were part of vernacular speech: "May the earth not receive you," "May the ground not consume you," "May the black earth spew you up," "May you remain incorrupt", "May the ground reject you." These were feared as condemning the cursed person to become a vampire.[34] A self-invoked curse might also have this dreaded result, as when a man, perjuring himself, called down on his own head all manner of damnation if what he said were false.

Maniotes believed that only after vengeance was taken against a murderer could the victim rest. An Arcadian belief was that: "When people died of a contagious disease, and no one would go near them, and they buried them without a priest and without a blessing, they become *vrykolakes*."[35] On Mytilene it was believed those who had committed great crimes, those who beat their parents, drunkards and suicides would become vampires.[36] On Syros and in Thrace it was the unburied and unbaptised.[37] Great sinners could become vampires, criminals whose evil deeds had never been discovered, those who stole from a church, drunkards, and people who had made five-finger signs at others. Most importantly, someone attacked by a vampire would himself, in turn, become a vampire.

At some time, the Church authorities must have adapted this superstition to their account, in order to terrorize those who defied its authority; for as late as the eighteenth century it was widely believed that those who died under a ban of excommunication become vampires.[38]

The Benedictine Abbot, Augustine Calmet, in his book on magic, witchcraft, and superstition, reported a striking experiment made at Constantinople in the fifteenth century, at the instance of the Sultan, to test the contention of the Greeks, that the bodies of those who had died under excommunication would not decay in the grave. The Patriarch caused the grave of a woman to be opened who had been excommunicated because of a scandal with an archbishop. The body was found intact, but blackened and swollen. It was then enclosed in a chest, which was locked and sealed with the Sultan's own private seal. The Patriarch then offered up prayers for the deceased, and formally revoked the sentence of excommunication. Three days later, the chest was opened, and it was found that the body had turned into dust.[39]

The religious authorities were, however, in something of a quandary over this power. On the one hand, they were anxious to maintain popular belief in the power of excommunication as a punitive weapon in their hands; yet at the same time, they were reluctant to be held responsible for deliberately creating such horrors. This led to rather scholastic distinctions being drawn between several different types of uncorrupted bodies. A ruling made at Thessaloniki listed four types of uncorrupted bodies with their causes. He who had left a command of his parents unfulfilled, or who was under their curse, had only the front portions of his body preserved. He who was under an anathema looked yellow, and his fingers were wrinkled. He who appeared white had committed some sin for which the penalty was excommunication. He who appeared to be bloated and black had been formally excommunicated by a bishop.[40]

Yet there were also known to be some other bizarre reasons why a body might not decay. An informant told Blum and Blum: "a girl committed suicide. She was a hairdresser and drank some medicines that she used for the hair, and she died. Her body did not dissolve. Some say this is because she committed the crime of suicide; others say it was that her body was poisoned by the medicines, and the worms didn't like the taste of the meat."[41]

In a similar story told to Sir Paul Ricaut, British Ambassador at Constantinople during the latter half of the seventeenth century, by a monk, named Sophronius, who had himself witnessed what he described on the island of Milos, the power of the Church was also demonstrated. The inhabitants had been for a long time disturbed by a nocturnal apparition, which was supposed to emanate from the grave of a man who had died excommunicated. The grave was opened, and the body found to be intact, with the veins full of blood. The monks of the island conferred, and decided that the proper course of action was to cut up the body and boil it in wine. The relatives of the deceased, however, succeeded in having the execution of this verdict postponed, and sent to Constantinople to implore the Patriarch to revoke the excommunication. Meanwhile, the body was placed in the Church, where prayers were offered for the repose of its soul. One day Sophronius himself was directing the ceremonies, when a sudden crack was heard in the coffin. It was opened, and discovered that the body was consumed away. The hour of this event was noted, and when the deputation returned from Constantinople, it was discovered that it coincided precisely with the time when the patriarch had lifted the dead man's sentence.[42]

Oddly, it was generally thought that only Christians suffered from the possibility of becoming vampires. It was held that Turks who become vampires would appear as dogs, cats,[43] or *smerdakia*.[44] In Macedonia, in the district of Melenik, in the middle of the twentieth century, G. F. Abbott encountered a belief which he described as one which, "though not quite so general at present as it used to be, cannot be considered extinct yet." This was the idea that Turks who had led a particularly wicked life would turn into wild boar at the moment of their death. The ring worn by a man on his finger, still on one of the boar's forefeet, would enable identification. It was said that the Turk would first begin to grunt like a pig, fall on all fours, rush out of the house grunting, and flee towards open country. At night, he would revisit the houses of his relatives, friends and acquaintances, and terrorise all those he encountered for forty days. When this period was over, he would withdraw to the mountains as a wild beast.[45]

There was significant disagreement about the appearance of a vampire when it had left its tomb.

In some places, vampires were indistinguishable from ordinary people in appearance, and could mingle among the living without detection for some considerable time.

Late one evening, a man named George Nouaros was preparing to go to sleep near a stove in his barn, in the countryside of Karpathos, some miles from his home in the village of Othous, when he noticed that his cow began staring fixedly at the door and bellowing. He was astonished, because his animal had never behaved in such a manner before. He raised his lamp and looked into the shadows, alarmed to see that the cow was trembling, its tail standing erect, and pawing with its front paws on the ground, all the while staring fixedly at the doors, as though it was afraid of something fearful. Nouaros muttered a prayer and made the sign of the cross. He was looking carefully around, throwing the light of the lamp into different corners of the barn, but could see nothing out of the ordinary, when there was a loud knocking on the door. "Who is it?" he cried. "Me!" a familiar voice replied. It was the *protopappas*, his partner in his craft. He ran to open the door, and saw his friend standing outside. "What's the matter? He asked. "Why are you on the road at this time of night?" "We have to go to the village, quickly, he said, " our other partner is very ill." "Sit down for a moment," Nouaros said, "while I saddle up my mule." "It doesn't matter," the other replied, "I will wait here at the door." Nouaros lost no time, and his mule was soon saddled and he was ready to go. Just before mounting, he picked up a small burning brand from the stove. "What do you want that for?" the protopappas said. "It bothers me." "What do you think," replied Nouaros. "On a dark night like this we need something to show us the road, or else we shall have an accident."

They sent out into the darkness. But the *protopappas* first held on to the mule's tail, and nearly unseated Nouaros. Then he went in front, refusing to let the mule walk by itself, and at one point grabbed the bridle, and tried to led them towards the cliff, saying that it was a shorter road. Another time he dragged them to the outside of the path over a ravine, so that the rider could see the tops of the mountains. They went along the

119

steep mountainside like a whirlwind. Nouaros thought that the *protopappas* was drunk, and began to fear for his life. But what could he do? The man was his partner. Several times, the *protopappas* complained about the torch Nouaros was carrying, and asked him to throw it away. And always he hastened on into the darkness, as though seeking to get away from its light. Finally, after much anguish, fear and dread on Nouaros' part, they arrived in the village.

As they passed through the streets, the *protopappas* fell behind, and seemed more subdued. Nouaras just assumed that his friend had sobered up. When they arrived at the church of the *Panayia*, outside which was then the cemetery, they stopped. The *protopappas* disappeared inside the cemetery. Nouaros called out "Where have you gone?" He dismounted and watered his mule at the spring there. His friend had disappeared altogether, so after waiting for a while, he decided to go home. When he knocked on the door of his house, his wife called out from inside "Who is it at this time of night?" "It's me, George," he replied, and the door opened. "What are you doing on the road at this time of night, his wife asked alarmed. When he explained about the *protopappas* his wife turned pale. "But he died today!" she cried.

It is said how all that night the dogs howled in the village; and that Nouaros was so shocked that he became ill for a very long time, and never entirely recovered his spirits after this shock.[46]

Dorothy Lee reported a story of a shepherd with a habit of going out at night. One night the moon was full, and it was bright like daylight. On his walk he saw in the distance a man wearing a *foustanella,* or Greek kilt. He thought nothing of it, although he had been told that he should not go that way at night. The two met, and when they did, instead of greeting him, the man whinnied. The shepherd looked at him, but said nothing. He went on a little way and looked back behind him, and the man had vanished. This was the *vrykolakas* who, they had told him, frequently came out in that place. He had been murdered, and when he was lying there dead before they found him and buried him, a mule had passed over his body, and he became a *vrykolakas*. The shepherd never passed that way again.[47]

Blum and Blum were told the story of a man who died and returned to human society, but to a different village, where he was not known, and where he got married, even though he had already been married in his own village. In his new home he plied his old trade of cobbler. He had two children by his second wife, but after a time some people from his home village who were visiting there, saw him and recognized who he was.

They went to his new wife and asked about him. She told them that he ate only liver, and that every Saturday he went away, to return again on Monday morning. Learning this, the villagers went to the grave, found the hole that he was using to emerge from it, and poured in hot water and vinegar. On doing this, they distinctly heard him complaining, from underground, about being burned.[48] (Vampires showed a strange preference for the trade of shoemaker or cobbler.)

When another man died, during the nights following his death, he continued to visit his wife and to sleep with her. From their intercourse two children were born. The woman used to leave the house early in the morning, visit friend's houses, and return home in the evening, when she discussed the village gossip with her husband. Usually the topic of the conversation was about couples who were having intercourse out of wedlock. Once she told her husband that she had heard about a best man sleeping with the bride after her husband had left the village. This shocked the vampire so much that he cried out: "This world is too immoral, let the earth swallow all of us now. At that moment, the entire family disappeared.[49]

In most parts of Greece, however, vampires were usually horribly recognizable. On Alonissos they had black flesh which gleamed in the darkness. On Mount Pelion they glowed in the dark. On the Saronic islands they were hunchbacked with black hands and long nails. On Tinos they had long beards, long hair, and long, crooked nails. On Lesbos they had wild, deep red faces, long teeth like wolves, dogs or cats, and sometimes went about on all fours, howling like a wolf.[50] Some Thracians pictured them as having the skin of a goat, a trunk like an elephant, and a single cyclopean eye.[51]

Vampires might also change shape. According to an American informant: A young man set off to go from his village to the town of Karytaina. When he went to cross the river Alphaeos, there was no bridge, only stones. He thought that the water was shallow and that he could jump from stone to stone. But by ill luck, he slipped and drowned. For days they sought after him, and finally they found his body, brought him back to the village and buried him. From the day that he was buried, he was a *vrykolakas*. He would go to the house and destroy whatever they had — flour and other things. He even had the power to go by day, to where his brother was, who had many sheep. He would go and call his name where the sheep had been left in the shade. When the people could have no peace any more because of him, they performed litanies, but with no result. One evening he went to his own house, so the following night his brother pondered over what to do, and finally he decided to shoot him. When, after two or three days, another noise was heard in the house, this man fired. After that, the *vrykolakas* would not go to the house any more. But he did go out in the pastures, to the sheep, and continued to do the same things that he had been doing before. Then one evening it began to thunder. Lightning struck a tree outside the house and killed a dog. From that moment onwards *vrykolakas* disappeared. Apparently the *vrykolakas* was in the dog; and the lightning had burnt him, whereas his brother's gun had been unable to stop him.[52]

Rarely, and rather inconsistently, the body of a vampire, when he walked abroad, was thought to be incorporeal. An American immigrant said: "He has exactly the body of a man such as he had before death. But he is only a phantasm. He is only like a kind of air. He has no tangible body."[53]

There was considerable divergence about *when* vampires walked. On Thasos, they appeared mostly in dreams. In Kalymnos they preferred cold, wintry nights with the north wind blowing. In Macedonia they walked on the night of the full moon. On Samos they also walked for a time after twelve noon, but they could not stray far from their tombs. On Amorgos, they might walk abroad throughout the day.[54] Paul Lucas, in his *Voyage au Levant*, (1705) claimed that dead men were reported to roam around on Corfu even in broad daylight, entering houses and generally frightening people. The authorities would then exhume the body of the reported offender, cut it up into small pieces and burn them, which solved the problem.[55] For Thracians, vampires were condemned to roam the earth only for forty days after death, and again with the *kallikantzari* during the Twelve Nights of Christmas.[56]

There was equal disagreement about when they customarily rested in their graves. On Seriphos, vampires feared to leave their graves on a Tuesday. On Tinos, they always remained in their tombs on Fridays, and in Preveza, they never went out on a Sunday[57]; while in most of Greece, Saturday was their day of rest.[58]

Vampires could occasionally be extraordinarily benevolent. Lawson heard a story of one who returned to plough his former employer's fields at night, doubling the work done and almost killing the oxen, until jealous neighbours exhumed the *vrykolakas* and burned him.[59]

Perhaps it is not surprising, in view of this, that the popular attitude towards vampires could sometimes seem remarkably low key. Blum and

Blum record a story of a woman who died all alone and became a vampire. She used to return to her house each night to do all the chores, including baking the bread; then she would leave, but only after urinating on the bread. Their informant said that her cousin's father met this vampire one night, when she got on the horse he was riding, sitting right behind him. He was terrified but did not say a word. He just lit a cigarette, and eventually she disappeared. When people went to her grave they found a hole in it. To prevent her return they lit a fire in the hole. The priest read the exorcism over it, and the problem disappeared.[60]

Despite these stories of mild and harmless vampires, the *vrykolakas* was generally regarded as a ravenous predator. Sometimes they robbed eggs and cattle. On Karpathos they broke into churches and threw things about.[61] A vampire thirsting for blood would first "feed on his own," and afterwards range abroad, attacking any who took his fancy. A gradual decline in health and vitality would be attributed to the unseen but malignant agency of this terrifying creature. He might kill his victim outright, in order to feed on the liver. In addition, he might bring plagues to man and beast. Near his grave the grass would die and the flowers wither. Dogs would wander ominously about the streets howling in the night.

For this reason, a general fear of vampires could be all-pervasive, as on Chios, where the inhabitants were said to walk out at night only in couples for this reason. There, it was thought that vampires might knock on the door, or call for the door to be opened, and anyone who opened to it was doomed to be his victim. However, since it never knocked or called twice, the inhabitants prudently never answered a first summons at their door. But if it was repeated, they knew there was nothing to fear. As a result, no one ever answered the door on the first occasion.[62]

Such a *vrykolakas* was Patino, a merchant from Patmos who died on a business trip to Anatolia and then revived in his coffin while being shipped home. A sailor who sat on the coffin felt the body inside moving beneath him. He and his fellows opened it up and found the body to be intact. But they decided to nail it up again and say nothing. His wife had him buried with full honours, but he then began appearing in houses in the area, violently assaulting people and causing damage. Prayers and exorcisms were fruitless in stopping the haunting. Finally, after more than fifteen persons had died either of injuries from its attacks or of fright, Patino's body was ordered to be sent back to Anatolia. The thoroughly spooked sailors charged with its transport simply stopped on the first island they passed and burned it, which brought the matter to a close.[63]

Pashley recorded the following story during his travels in Crete. "Once on a time, the village of Kalikrati, in the district of Sfakia, was haunted by a *katakhanas* [vampire], and people did not know what man he was or from what part. This *katakhanas* destroyed both children and many full-grown men; and desolated both that village and many others. As he was a man of note, they had built an arch over his grave. Now, a certain shepherd who was a friend of his, so that they stood as godfather to each others' children, was tending his sheep and goats near the church. On being caught by a shower, he went, to the sepulchre to shelter from the rain. Afterwards, he determined to sleep, and spend the night there. After taking off his arms, he placed them by the stone which served him as his pillow cross wise.

During the night, then, as he wished to go out again that he might destroy men, the vampire said to the shepherd, "Get up, for I have some business that requires me to come out." The shepherd did not answer him not, either the first, second, or the third time: for he realised that the man had become a vampire, and that it was he who was responsible for all the evil things which had happened. So he said to him, on the fourth time of his speaking, I shall not get up from here, friend, for I fear that you may do me some mischief. But if I must get up, swear to me by your winding-sheet, that you will not hurt me, and after that I will get up. When it was clear that the shepherd would not let him get up, he swore as he wished. (This was the only oath of a vampire that could be trusted.) On this he got up, and, taking his arms, removed them away from the monument, and the vampire came up, and, greeting the shepherd, said to him, "You must not go away, but sit down here, for I have some business which I must go after; but I shall return within the hour, for I have something to say to you. So the shepherd waited for him.

The vampire went a distance of about ten miles, where there was a couple recently married, and destroyed them. On his return his friend saw that he was carrying some liver, his hands being moistened with blood; and, as he carried it, he blew into it, just as the butcher does, to increase its size. He showed his friend that it was cooked, as if it had been done on the fire. After this he said, "Let us sit down, that we may eat." The shepherd pretended to eat it, but only swallowed dry bread, and kept dropping pieces of the liver into his clothes. When the meal ended, the vampire said to the shepherd, "What you have seen you must not talk about, for if you do, my twenty nails will be fixed in your children and yourself."

Yet the shepherd lost no time in giving information to the priests and others. They went to the tomb, and found the vampire just as he had been buried. Everyone was satisfied that he was the one who was responsible for all the evil. So they collected a great deal of wood, and they cast him on top of it, and burnt him. His friend was not present, but when the vampire was half consumed, he too arrived in order that he might see the ceremony. The vampire cast a single spot of blood upon his foot, which wasted away as if it had been roasted on a fire. Because of this, they sifted even the ashes, and found the little finger-nail of the vampire unburned, and burned that too.[64]

Not surprisingly, a host of prophylactics were marshalled to protect against the depredations of these fearful predators. On Lesbos, a cross of reeds would be fixed behind the door. On Evia plates bearing the shape of the cross were placed on the walls. On many islands, a piece of pig's tongue would be nailed above the door with a nail taken from a coffin. On Santorini, they would seal the keyholes of the doors during the night with blessed bread from the churches. The Nisyrotes would carry a black handled knife previously blessed by a priest. The feisty Cretans would paint on their doors the insulting gesture of an open hand, palm out. In Macedonia, mustard seed would be spread over the roof, or the doors barricaded with briars and brambles.[65] On Mykonos they would incise a five-pointed star on their doors.[66] Lee records an interviewee saying: " . . . in our village, on the outside of the church, they had drawn—I never saw it—the outline of a wolf. And when anyone from another village became a *vrykolakas*, they would take earth from under the sketch of the wolf and would strew it all the way to the grave of the *vrykolakas*. And the wolf would go and eat the *vrykolakas*, and he would disappear.[67] Some believed that a wandering vampire could only be killed by gunpowder. Naturally, the sign of the cross was protection against their depredations when out of doors. When a vampire grabbed hold of the tail of the mule a country man was riding one evening on the road between Ioannina and Ktismata, he made the sign of the cross three times, and it vanished.[68]

To prevent a vampire from rising from its grave, a host of measures might also be employed: covering it with a new fishing net, fig wood, olive wood, onions, garlic, a pig's heart, quicklime, sulphur, salt water, boiling water, boiling oil, beating with a gravedigger's spade, rocks with crosses painted on them, ashes from a priest's hearth, or nailing the remains with an iron spit. In the old graveyard of Bourkoti on Andros, no burial is intact. Every corpse has been pierced through the heart by a black-handled knife. Pieces of the host, or consecrated communion bread, were sometimes put on the bodies or mouths of the dead.[69]

It was on the day that the vampire did not roam that suspect corpses would be exhumed. The burning of a body which had once been anointed with holy oil was strictly forbidden by the Church. For that reason, there is not a single crematorium in Greece to this day. Thus burning was only attempted as a last resource. If there was a suspected case of vampire haunting, people would often go to the grave with a priest, and there pray. After which the priest pour boiling water and vinegar onto the tomb.

Joseph Pitton de Tournefort recorded the detection and laying of a Maniote vampire:

"Passing by a dreary and half-deserted village, I was shown a house to which another wild legend attached, and which was said to have been once inhabited by a shoemaker's widow. Her husband, however, though dead, had not entirely departed; for, being a vampire, he used a vampire's privilege, and bursting the bondage of the tomb, returned every night except on the Saturday to his old abode, and sometimes even worked at his old trade. At length the woman became pregnant. The villagers taxed her with infidelity to her husband's memory, and she in her own defence maintained that she was on the point of giving birth to no unlawful issue.

At this horrifying disclosure the villagers sallied forth to attack the Vampire in his tomb, undertaking the enterprise on a Saturday morning, on which day alone the Vampire's devil-imparted strength forsakes him, and the grave has power to hold his body. They found him working in his grave, making shoes. 'How did you know that I was a Vampire?' exclaimed the still living tenant of the tomb. A villager, in answer, pointed to a youth whose cheek a month before had been bright with health, but on which the ghastly paleness of disease and coming death had fixed its mark. The Vampire immediately spat at him. The moisture from those accursed lips burnt the man's capote as though it had been fire, but it could not hurt the man himself, because it was the blessed Saturday. Maddened by the failure of his attempt, the Vampire imprudently cried, 'Though I am nerveless now, yet you shall taste my vengeance to the full on every night save this alone.' On hearing this alarming threat the neighbours fell upon him, tore him to pieces, and cut out his heart, dividing it into portions, and distributing the several parts among the villagers, commanding each one to eat his allotted fragment . . . - and this, is the only real specific against vampires; and since that event, no vampire has ever molested the village again, though for two months before persons had been perishing daily under their fatal influence."[70]

Tournefort was himself an eye-witness of the laying of a *Vrykolakas*, which haunted the island of Myconos, and whose body was not only transferred to the neighbouring; islet of St. George, but was there consumed with fire.

"We were present at a very different Scene, and one very barbarous, in the same Island, which happened upon occasion of one of those Corpses, which they fancy come to life again after their interment. The Man whose Story we are going to relate, was a Peasant of Mycone, naturally ill-natured and quarrelsome; this is a Circumstance to be taken notice of in such cases: he was murdered in the fields, no body knew how, or by whom. Two days after his being buried in a Chapel in the Town it was noised about that he was seen to walk in the night with great haste, that he tumbled about Peoples Goods, put out their Lamps, griped them behind and a thousand other monkey Tricks. At first the Story was received with Laughter; but the thing was looked upon to be Serious, when the better sort of People began to complain of it; the Papas themselves gave credit to the Fact, and no doubt had their reasons for so doing; Masses must be said, to be sure: but for all this, the Peasant drove his old trade, and heeded nothing they could do. After diverse meetings of the chief People of the City, or Priests and Monks, it was gravely concluded, that 'twas necessary, in consequence of some musty Ceremonial, to wait till nine days after the Interment should be expired.

On the tenth day they said one Mass in the Chapel where the Body was laid, in order to drive out the Demon which they imagined was got into it. After Mass, they took up the Body, and got every thing ready for pulling out its Heart. The butcher of the town, an old clumsy fellow, first opens the belly instead of the breast: he groped a long while among the entrails, but could not find what he looked for; at last somebody told him he should cut up the diaphragm. The heart was pulled out, to the admiration of all the spectators. In the mean time, the corpse stunk so abominably, that they were obliged to burn frankincense; but this smoke mixing with the exhalations from the carcass, increased the Stink, and began to muddle the poor peoples' pericranies. Their imagination, struck with the spectacle before them, grew full of visions. It came into their noddles, that a thick smoke arose out of the body; we durst not say it was the smoke of the incense. They were incessantly bawling out "Vroucalacas!" in the chapel and place before it: this is the name they give to these pretended redivivi. The noise bellowed through the streets, and it seemed to be a name invented on purpose to rend the roof of the chapel. Several there present averred, that the wretch's blood was extremely red: the butcher swore the body was still warm; whence they concluded, that the deceased was a very ill man for not being thoroughly dead, or in plain terms for suffering himself to be reanimated by Old Nick; which is the notion they have of a vroucolacas. They then roared out that name in a stupendous manner. Just at this time came in a flock of people, loudly protesting they plainly perceived the body was not grown stiff, when it was carried from the fields to church to be buried, and that consequently it was a true Vroucolacas; which word was still the burden of the song.

I don't doubt they would have sworn it did not stink, had we not been there; so amazed were the poor people with this disaster, and so infatuated with their notion of the dead's being reanimated. As for us who got as close to the corpse as we could, that we might be more exact in our observations, we were almost poisoned with the intolerable stink that issued from it. When they asked us what we thought of this body, we told them we believed it to be very thoroughly dead: but as we were willing to cure, or at least not to exasperate their prejudiced imaginations, we represented to them, that it was no wonder the butcher should feel a little warmth when he groped among the entrails that were then rotting; that it was no extraordinary thing for it to emit fumes, since dung turned up will do the same; that as for the pretended redness of the blood, it still appeared by the butcher's Hands to be nothing but a very stinking nasty smear.

After all our reasons, they were of opinion it would be their wisest course to burn the dead man's heart on the seashore: but this execution did not make him a bit more tractable; he went on with his racket more furiously than ever: he was accused of beating folks in the night, breaking down doors, and even roofs of houses; clattering windows; tearing clothes; emptying bottles and vessels. 'Twas a most thirsty devil! I believe he did not spare any body but the consul in whose house we lodged. Nothing could be more miserable than the condition of this island; all the inhabitants seemed frighted out of their senses; the wisest among them were stricken like the rest: 'twas an epidemical disease of the brain, as dangerous and infectious as the madness of dogs. Whole families quitted their houses, and brought their tent-beds from the farthest parts of town into the public place, there to spend the night. They were every instant complaining of some new insult; nothing was to be heard but sighs and groans at the approach of night: the better sort of people retired into the country.

When the prepossession was so general, we thought it our best way to hold our tongues. Had we opposed it, we had not only been accounted ridiculous blockheads, but atheists and infidels. How was it possible to stand against a madness of a whole people? Those that believed we doubted the truth of the fact, came and upbraided us with our incredulity, and strove to prove that there were such things as vroucolacasses, by citations out of the *Buckler of Faith*, written by F. Richard a Jesuit missionary. He was a Latin, say they, and consequently you ought to give him credit. We should have got nothing by denying the justness of the consequence: it was as good a comedy to us every morning, to hear the new follies committed by this night-bird; they charged him with being guilty of the most abominable sins.

Some citizens, that were zealous for the good of the public, fancied they had been deficient in the most material part of the ceremony. They were of opinion, that they had been wrong in saying Mass before they had pulled out the wretch's heart: had we taken this precaution, quoth they, we had bit the devil, as sure as a gun; he would have been hanged before he would ever have come there again: whereas saying mass first, the cunning dog fled it for a while, and came back again when the danger was over.

Notwithstanding these wise reflections, they remained in as much perplexity as they were the first day: they meet night and morning, they debate, they make processions three days and three nights; they oblige the papas to fast; you might see them running from house to house, holy-water-brush in hand, sprinkling it all about, and washing the doors with it; nay, they poured it into the mouth of the poor *vroucolacas*.

We so often repeated it to the magistrates of the town, that in Christendom we should keep the strictest watch a-nights upon such an occasion, to observe what was done; that at last they caught a few vagabonds, who undoubtedly had a hand in these disorders: but either they were not the chief ringleaders, or else they were released too soon. For two days afterwards, to make themselves amends for the Lent they had kept in prison, they fell foul again upon the wine-tubs of those who were such fools as to leave their houses empty in the night: so that the people were forced to betake themselves again to their prayers.

One day, as they were hard at this work, after having stuck I know not how many naked swords over the grave of this corpse, which they took up three or four times a day, for any man's whim; an Albaneze that happened to be at Mycone, took upon him to say with a voice of authority, that it was to the last degree ridiculous to make use of the swords of Christians in a case like this. Can you not conceive, blind as ye are, says he, that the handles of these swords, being made like a cross, hinders the devil from coming out of the body? Why do you not rather take the Turkish sabres? The advice of this learned man had no effect: the vroucolacas was incorrigible, and all the inhabitants were in a strange consternation; they knew not now what saint to call upon, when of a sudden with one voice, as if they had given each other the hint, they fell to bawling out all through the city, that it was intolerable to wait any longer; that the only way left was to burn the vroucolacas entire; that after so doing, let the devil lurk in it if he could; that 'twas better to have recourse to this extremity, than to have the island totally deserted. And indeed whole families began to pack up, in order to retire to Syra or Tinos. The magistrates therefore ordered the vroucolacas to be carried to the point of the island St. George, where they prepared a great pile with pitch and tar, for fear the wood, as dry as it was, should not burn fast enough of itself. What they had before left of this miserable carcass was thrown into this fire, and consumed presently. It was on the first of January 1701. We saw the flame as we returned from Delos. It might justly be called a bonfire of joy, since after this no more complaints were heard against the vroucolacas; they said that the devil had now met with his match, and some ballads were made to turn him into ridicule.[71]

In the mid-twentieth century, G. R. Abbott was informed about a case of vampirism in Alistrati, a village between Serres and Drama, which had occurred shortly before he arrived in Macedonia. The corpse was taken out of the grave and scalded with boiling oil, and pierced through the navel with a long nail. Then the grave was covered over with earth, and millet seed scattered over it. The idea of the scattered seed was that the vampire, if still active, would spend hours trying to gather the seed, and had only between about ten at night and cockcrow to do their mischief.[72] If such methods proved insufficient, then the body must be burned, but this was done only as a last resort, because of the belief that a body hallowed by the baptismal chrism should not be burned.[73] Occasionally, even the Turks would resort to this method to get rid of a Christian vampire.[74]

Orthodox bishops at times struggled hard to put down such superstitions, though not always with success. Tournefort records that not one priest would be at St. George when the body of the Mykonos vampire was burnt, for fear the bishop should exact a sum of money of them, for taking up and burning a corpse without permission from him.

By Bent's time, the burning of vampires had generally ceased, except in northern Andros. Instead, the priest would go to the grave and pray for the soul of the dead person, and then pour boiling water and vinegar into the grave. It was claimed by many that as the priest did this, they could hear the rattle of settling bones under the ground.[75]

When the old monk, Barba Manthos, in Keos, met another islander, Manetos, on the road, some time after his death, he had the parishioners open his grave. There was no body inside, so they got the priest. He poured in oil and set fire to it. Barba Manthis said that he saw a blue flame shoot up into the sky; but it must have been successful, because Manetos was never seen again.[76]

People born on a Saturday were reckoned to have some power over vampires. At Lyakkovikia someone born on a Saturday had a familiar spirit in the form of a dog which followed him about after dark, and drove away vampires. A native of Sochos assured Abbott that he had lured a vampire into a barn, kept him there preoccupied in counting the grains in a pile of millet, and while he was thus engaged, had nailed him to the wall.[77] This may be compared with attempts to "nail" the plague, above.[78]

On Skyros they would carry the body around forty churches in turn and then reinter it. In many other places, they would inter it on an uninhabited islet, believing that the vampire could not cross salt water.[79] On Rhodes, when a woman returned in this form, one of the dead woman's shifts was laid on the ground. Assisted by two men who held on to him, lest the vampire return and seize him, the village priest walked backwards and forwards over the neck of the garment reading prayers. The shift swelled up and split. This was the point when the spirit escaped through the opening, and the vampire was laid.[80]

On Milos the infamous Kouvelos became a vampire by cursing himself when dying. Next day, his brother was found strangled with black finger-marks on his neck. The prayers of the clergy failed to stop the dead man's prowlings, so he was exhumed. The body was black in the face, the hair long and wild, the finger nails grown long, and soiled with the blood of his victims. They cut out his heart, burned it, and scattered it to the winds. Then they tied up the rest of his body in a sack and threw it into the sea. Such was the wash when the corpse touched the water that the boat was nearly swamped.[81]

Perhaps one of the most unusual reasons for the successful laying of a vampire appears in the following tale: A moneylender of Santorini named Ianettis, reformed in the last year of his life, died asking his wife to pay his remaining debts, which she failed to do. Ianettis began haunting his village with poltergeist-like activity: pulling the bedclothes off of sleepers, emptying wine kegs, and generally abusing and terrorizing people. He visited the Mother Prioress of a Dominican convent, awakened her by rolling her rosary on the floor, jeered at her prayers and threw her shoes into the water cistern. His body was finally exhumed, and was only partially decayed. It was exorcised for a full day and then dismembered and reinterred, but the *vrykolakas'* activity still did not stop, until his wife reluctantly made good his debts.[82]

The islanders appear to have been especially fearful of vampires. Hydra is said to have been infected with them, until a zealous bishop succeeded in transferring them all to the island of Kamena, just off the coast of Santorini. Since it was believed that vampires could not cross salt water by their own power, it was customary for the priest to exhume them on the day of the week when it was believed that they rested in their graves, place the remains in a sack, and tip them out on an uninhabited islet especially reserved for that purpose.[83] The people of Mytilene would bury those who would not lie quietly in their graves on an adjacent uninhabited island.[84] The islet of Brykastro off Kythnos,[85] St.George's and Vaou off Mykonos,[86] Lagos off Methona, in Lesvos, and Kalathas off Chania, were set aside as a place of burial for vampires. Other vampire graveyards include Ay. Phokas off Monemvasia, Nekro and Nekrothikes off Kalymnos, Leipsoi off Patmos, Daimonopetra off Ikaria, Diavololimano off Samos, Dimononisia off Karpathos, etc.[87]

Occasionally, fear of vampires could generate a general panic.

Father Francois Richard, in his *Relation de l'Isle de Sant-erini*, (1657) wrote that the devil keeps certain bodies incorrupt and animates them. Under his command they are able to wander around, enter houses, strike people mute with fear, and assault them, even killing them. When a village is beset by such a *vrykolakas* . . . they huddle together all in one house for protection, and apply to their bishop for permission to exhume the suspect. This is done on a day when a *vrykolakas* rests in its grave. If the body is found "fresh and gorged with new blood", it is "exorcised" with prayer until it dissolves before their eyes. If prayer is ineffective, the body is cremated.

Xavie Scofani reported that on Euboia in 1791 vampires were responsible for a widespread epidemic. The dead were disinterred, and any found whole pierced through the heart with a red-hot iron spit.[88]

Three men from Sofikos, in Korinthia, once went to the village of Korfo looking for work. There they got drunk and took a boat out to sea. They were drowned in a sudden storm during the night, and their bodies were washed up on the coast. Their families gathered up the bodies and buried them outside the wall of the fold at Sofiko, because the priest considered them suicides and would not bury them in consecrated ground with the rites of the church.

During the next few nights, the villagers were awakened by loud noises: stamping feet, bumps, cracking sounds, noisy scratching, and inarticulate lamentations. During the hours of darkness, the terrified people would gather together for safety in the central houses of the community. When they returned to their homes at daybreak they would find furniture disarranged, and fire damage from flaming darts thrown in all directions. The general opinion was that vampires were responsible, and that it was the recently buried men who were causing the problem. The tombs were opened, and the corpses taken to the tiny islet of Sideronas, in the Saronic Gulf, which was used as a graveyard for suspected vampires, where they tied a rock to each one and threw them into the sea. On the next day, however, they washed up on the shore with the remains of the frayed ropes. It was decided that more serious measures would have to be taken. They plucked out the hearts, hacked the bodies to pieces, burned them, and scattered the ashes at sea.[89]

Nicholas Dragoumis recalled, in his memoirs, a cholera epidemic in Naxos during the early 1930s, which carried off a great number of victims. The rumour circulated that the Naxian dead in the other world were so numerous that they had ganged together, overpowered Charos, and were coming back to earth to take possession of their own. The fear was so great that the inhabitants rushed home at sunset, barred their doors and windows, and piled the furniture against them. But this was often in vain, for the spectres entered through the keyholes and scared the living for many an anxious day.[90]

Occasionally a bishop would try to suppress the problem entirely. "About the commencement of the [nineteenth] century, the Metropolitan bishop of Larissa received advice of a papas having disinterred two bodies, and thrown them into the Haliacmon, on pretence of their being *Vrukolakes*. Upon being summoned before the bishop, the priest confessed the fact, and asserted in justification, that a report prevailed of a large animal having been seen to issue, accompanied with flames, out of the grave in which the two bodies had been buried. The bishop began by obliging the priest to pay him two hundred and fifty piastres; (his holiness did not add that he made over the money to the poor.) - By then publishing, throughout the diocese, that any similar offence would be punished with double the fine and certain loss of station, the bishop effectually quieted all the vampires of his episcopal province."[91]

In some areas, belief in vampires survived well into the twentieth century, as is illustrated by the following story of events in 1922, which took place in Pyrgos. A young husband, suffering from depression, hanged himself. He was excommunicated as a suicide, and buried outside the churchyard, despite pleas from his widow, who became withdrawn and silent. After two months, the village experienced poltergeist-like activity: people reported their beds being shaken and the sensation of being bitten at night, after which they became ill. In the course of a week, two people died. Then the suicide's widow confessed to the priest that her dead husband had been making conjugal visits to her during that time. The dead man was pronounced a *vrykolakas*, and plans were made to exhume him, dismember his body, remove his heart and burn the remains. The body was found shrivelled, hardened and covered with skin, with its heart still beating. It was burned, but the story concludes with the widow giving birth to a monstrous baby, which died at birth. In short, this folktale includes nearly every detail from the various *vrykolakas* traditions, and according to the author, was still being repeated "as fact" in Pyrgos in the mid-1970's.[92]

The most eminent writer on the subject of Greek vampires was Leo Allatius. Born on the island of Chios in 1586, he had a distinguished career in the Roman Catholic Church, during which he travelled extensively. He defined a vampire thus: "The vrykolakas is the body of a man who has led a wicked and debauched life, very often of one who has been excommunicated by his Bishop. Such bodies do not like other corpses suffer decomposition after burial or fall to dust . . . a skin of extreme toughness becomes swollen and distended all over, so that the joints can barely be bent; the skin becomes stretched like the parchment of a drum, and when struck gives out the same noise".

As a boy, Allatius had witnessed the opening of the tomb of an alleged vampire on Chios. He reported: "the skin was stretched tight, hard, and livid . . . the face was covered with crisp, dark hair, but the head was partly bald, and a little hair appeared on the limbs which were smooth; so swollen was the trunk that the arms had been forced out on either side; the hands were open, the eyelids drooped, the mouth gaped wide with sharp, gleaming teeth" He initiated the systematic study of the phenomenon in Greece.

Many highly descriptive terms were used for the corpse of a vampire: "timpanios", which denotes the tight, drum-like skin of a bloated corpse; on Kithnos, "Alitos", unsolvable or indissoluble; in Cyprus, Katakhanas, the "destroyer", in Tenos as the "snatcher". The word *vrykolakas*, and its variants is undoubtedly of Slavonic origin, being found in Bohemia, Dalmatia, Montenegro, Servia, and Bulgaria. It appears as Vilkolak among the Poles, with the signification rather of were-wolf. It has therefore been suggested that belief in vampires is a foreign introduction into Greece during the Slavic invasions which began in 587.[93]

That vampires are Greek in origin, however, is rendered likely by the fact that in the islands, which were never subjected to Slavic influence, and where fear of the vampire was perhaps keenest felt, they were known by purely Greek names.[94] Certainly, there are many accounts, in ancient literature, of dead souls requiring blood to regain their vitality. Lawson reports that oaths are found in Greek literature binding both the speaker and others to being rejected by the earth, being turned out of Hades by Tantalus, and of remaining incorruptible after death. Thus Euripides' Hippolytus says to his father, "in death may neither sea nor earth receive my flesh, if I have proved false." Lawson argues that bodily return was expected and feared in the case of blood-guilt and vengeance. He points out that in ancient times murderers frequently mutilated their victims by cutting off their hands and feet and tucking them under the corpse's armpits, or binding them to its chest with a band to prevent the murdered victim from returning bodily to avenge itself on the murderer. One rationale for this is that such mutilation character of these Avengers approximates very closely to that of the modern *vrykolakes*. True, there is one fundamental difference; the ancient Avenger directed his wrath solely against the author of his sufferings . . . the modern *vrykolakas* is unreasoning in his wrath and plagues indiscriminately all who fall in his way.[95] He lists the many qualities that Avengers and *vrykolakes* share. Modern stories there are in plenty, which tell how the *vrykolakas* springs upon his victim and rends him and drinks his blood; how sheer terror of his aspect has driven men mad; how, in order to escape him, whole families have been driven forth from their native island to wander in exile; how death has often been the issue of his assaults; and how those whom a *vrykolakas* has slain become themselves *vrykolakes*.

Thus, long before the arrival of either the Slavs or Christianity, the ancient Greeks believed that a person could be trapped indefinitely in its body, if the body could not dissolve and free the soul from the earth, and so be forever doomed to roam trapped, yearning or ravening, between life and death. The only release was the forced "dissolution" of cremation. Lawson concludes that all revenants were originally called, *alastores*, "Wanderers"; but subsequently that name was restricted only to the vengeful class of revenants. It seems clear that only the name was introduced by the Slavonic immigrants, for we find the vampire in places where the Slavs never penetrated, such as Crete, and the islands of the Aegean as far as Rhodes and Cyprus.

John Cuthbert Lawson has argued that inconsistencies he detects in the modern belief in vampires can be explained by the conflation of two different traditions. He held that the original Greek belief was in revenants, who generally behaved in a reasonable way when they returned from the dead, although men who had been murdered might seek revenge. At the same time, there lingered in certain regions the ancient tradition of the werewolf, the living man transformed into a ravening monster. With the introduction of Slavic traditions, came the idea that werewolves, when they die, become vampires, and these revenants could be distinguished by their ferocity, since their behaviour after death was no more rational than it would have been when they were alive. This class of revenants became distinguished for their bloodthirsty character. Then by the seventeenth century, the memory of the milder revenants had faded, and all embodied revenants came to be regarded as predatory and violent.[96]

Vampires became common in modern literature following the publication of *Dracula* by the Irish writer Bram Stoker in 1897, who located his vampires in Transylvania. However, it had been preceded by several other romantic works of fiction with similar themes, which suggested a Greek origin for the literary tradition. The Greek doctor, and acquaintance of Lord Byron, John Polidouri, had written *The Vampyre* in 1817. Later, in 1847, James Malcolm Raimer had written *Varney the Vampire or The Feast of Blood*, the tale of a journey to the vampire-haunted island of Skyros.

Rational explanations for belief in vampires may lie in the inexact and hasty diagnosis of death in Greece until modern times, coupled with the practice of exhuming corpses after three years, when evidence of premature burial might have been misinterpreted.

Mistaking coma for death seems to have been an ever-present possibility before the advent of modern medicine. Thus an informant told researchers that on her mother's island a man who was very ill became unconscious. The people thought he had died, and so they prepared his funeral. After the ceremony, a movement was spotted in the coffin and the man slowly began to arise. The people present jumped to the conclusion that he was already becoming a vampire, and in their fright they threw everything they could find at him, both sticks and rocks, and killed him.[97]

The common practice, before the present century, was to bury people within twenty-four hours of death. A visitor to Athens in the 1890s, Samuel J. Barrows, tells how one morning a man in the neighbourhood of his lodging shot himself. A short while later, two of the visitor's friends went on an excursion to Marathon. When they got back, in time for an early dinner, Barrows observed that the dead man had already been buried for several hours.[98] This must have compounded the chance of being buried alive. When the bodies were exhumed after three years, signs that the corpse had moved in the grave would no doubt be considered as indications of vampirism.

Another story told to Richard and Eva Blum illustrates the tragedies which could result from the combination of lack of medical knowledge with speedy burial and superstition. The grandfather of their informant had been a doctor on one of the islands. When a girl there became unconscious and in a coma, people thought that she was dead. The doctor tried to explain that she was still alive, and might yet be saved with proper treatment, but the parents became upset. They said that she was dead, and if he revived her she would be a vampire. So in spite of his pleas, they buried her. Later that night he went to the graveyard alone, and dug her up. Her breathing was very weak, but she was still alive. But she died in his arms.[99]

The earl of Caernarvon was no doubt correct in his surmise that in the atmosphere of belief, "Every case of gradual decline was attributed to the unseen but malignant agency of this terrific creature of the imagination; the man worn out by real physical disease was startled from his unrefreshing sleep . . . and, convinced in the growing weakness of his sinking frame, that he could count the precious drops of blood of which he had that night been drained."[100]

In any event, it is clear that the common Greek practice of digging up corpses three years after burial in order to store the bones in an ossuary must have been a spur to the superstition of vampirism, for there are many reasons why a body might not be entirely dissolved. Among those which might operate today are the chemicals taken in by those receiving chemotherapy for cancer. In addition, hair and nails continue to grow after death for some time, producing a horrific appearance if the body has not dissolved.

[1] Alexiou 37.
[2] Alexiou 38.
[3] Lawson
[4] Fermor (1) 70.
[5] Bent 176.
[6] Stewart 53: Νουαρου 248.
[7] Ναουράου 248.
[8] Fermor (1) 69.
[9] McNall 69.
[10] Πολίτη 2:232.
[11] Fermor (1) 67.
[12] Μαντζουράνι.
[13] Τσικλίδης (2) 1:281.
[14] Δορμπαράκης και Πανουτσοπούλου 395.
[15] Durrell 113-4.

[16] Τσικλίδης 2:53

[17] Τσικλίδης (2) 1:229.

[18] Tomkinson (3) 123.

[19] Tomkinson (4) 29-30.

[20] Abbott 258.

[21] Bent 23.

[22] Γιαννουλάκης (3) *passim*.

[23] Πολίτη 1:190.

[24] Tomkinson (3) 110-1.

[25] Γαλλοπούλου 250.

[26] Ορφανουδάκης 501-5.

[27] Edwards 358.

[28] Lee.

[29] Blum & Blum 75.

[30] Durrell 140.

[31] Γιαννουλάκης (2) 376.

[32] Blum & Blum 74ff.

[33] Abbott 219.

[34] Blum & Blum 75.

[35] Lee.

[36] Γιαννουλάακης (2) 376.

[37] Γιαννουλάκης (2) 376.

[38] Rodd 195.

[39] Rodd 193.

[40] Lawson 370.

[41] Blum & Blum, 76.

[42] Rodd 193-4.

[43] Stewart 187.

[44] Πολίτη 2:315.

[45] Abbott 215-6.

[46] Νουάρου 250-2.

[47] Lee.

[48] Blum & Blum 74.

[49] Blum & Blum 72.

[50] Γιαννουλάκης (2) 377.

[51] Θρακιώτης 301.

[52] Τσικλίδης (2) 2:202

[53] Lee.

[54] Γιαννουλάκης (2) 377.

[55] Lawson 371.

[56] Θρακιώτης, 301.

[57] Γιαννουλάκης (2) 375.

[58] Rodd 193.

[59] Lawson 370.

[60] Blum & Blum 71.

[61] Νουάρου 249.

[62] Rodd 192; Γιαννουλακης (2) 376.

[63] Lawson 368.

[64] Pashley 2:197-200.
[65] Abbott 219.
[66] Βούρνας και Γαρίδη 184.
[67] Lee.
[68] Παπακωνσταντίνου 348.
[69] Γιαννουλάκης (2) 379.
[70] Pitton de Tournefort 1:142-3
[71] Pitton de Tournefort 1:103-7
[72] Abbott 218-9.
[73] Pashley 2:202.
[74] Pashley 2:202, n.17.
[75] Bent 23.
[76] Bent 223.
[77] Abbott 221.
[78] See page 97.
[79] Lawson 372.
[80] Newton 212-3.
[81] Καναράκης 411.
[82] Lawson 369.
[83] Rodd 194; Pashley 2:203.
[84] Newton 213.
[85] Bent 213.
[86] Βούρνας και Γαρίδη 185
[87] Γιαννουλάκης (2) 380.
[88] Γιαννουλάκης (2) 379.
[89] Τσικλίδης (2) 1:198-9.
[90] Rodd 190-1.
[91] Pashley 2:205.
[92] Konstantinos, 52-58.
[93] e.g. Rodd 188-9, 384.
[94] Abbott 218.
[95] Lawson, 458.
[96] Lawson 384ff.
[97] Blum & Blum 71-2.
[98] Seymour, reprinted in Tomkinson (5) 414.
[99] Blum & Blum 72.
[100] Caernarvon 164.

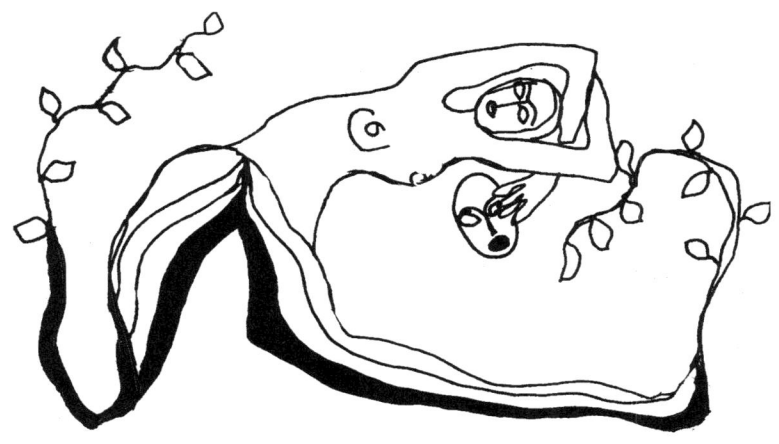

Phantoms

In the mid-twentieth century, the inhabitants of Vassilika, a village in the valley of the river Anthemos, would talk about a phenomenon they called the "Passage". It was a rush of wind which, suddenly rising from the Well of Murat at one end of the settlement, swept furiously through the village and then as suddenly sank into the Tomb of Ali on the edge of a watercourse at the other end. As it sped along, it filled the countryside with horrible noises, which sometimes were like the bellowing of cattle, sometimes like the bleating of goats or the grunting of pigs, and often like the shrieks and wails of human beings. It blasted everything it blew upon. Whoever happened to be caught by its blighting breath would instantly struck dumb. Some of the peasants boasted of having followed these mysterious sounds, and affirmed that they ceased abruptly at the Tomb of Ali.

An old woman of the village assured G. F. Abbott "in the most confident and confidential manner imaginable" that her own father once saw, amid the whirlwind and the clouds of dust it raised, a child carrying a pitcher on either shoulder, a feat of which an ordinary child was incapable. He pursued the apparition down to the riverside and there lost sight of it as it vanished.[1]

Such *phantasmata,* or "appearances", were the least stable of the *exotika.* They appeared in various forms, sometimes as humans, sometimes as animals, or even as inanimate objects.[2] They were thought to be *aerika,* spirits of the air, too intangible and vague to be clearly defined. Such was the *Hamodrakas* of Milos, a spirit of no particular form which would often jump out before travellers at crossroads.[3]

Weird natural phenomena seem quite common in Greece. Laurence Durrell once knew an Austrian botanist, Egon Kahr, who was searching for a particular rock plant on the central mountain of Lefkas, and gazing out over the famous White Cliffs, when he suddenly became enveloped in a white sea mist, which condensed into a shape with a definite outline. Inside he could hear strange sounds, such as the mewing of seagulls and disembodied human voices. Not surprisingly, he fled. But perhaps he did not flee far enough, because a few months later he was killed when he fell from a tall apartment building in Athens, and was found on the pavement still clutching a telephone in his hand, which had been wrenched from the wall.[4]

A peasant at Galatista, in the Chalcidic Peninsula, who was known as "Crook-Neck," was said to owe his deformity to a similarly inexplicable incident. One evening, as he was walking home from the fields, he perceived what he took to be a harmless, though erring, goat, browsing in a meadow. He approached it and was lifting the animal on his shoulder, with the intention of taking it as a present to his wife, when it just melted into space, leaving its captor his deformity as a lasting souvenir of the incident. Another peasant told Abbott that he one day alighted with his comrades under a fig-tree which stood close to a holy spring dedicated to Ayia Paraskevi. All of a sudden a ball of cotton-wool sprang up from the ground and rolled down the slope. They pursued it until it stopped and shot up into a white column. There it stood for a while and then disappeared.[5]

In a spot outside the town of Argos a pair of dogs, one black and one white, run past at midnight. At Loviarika at Limena a sow and her piglets pass through. If the sow is chased, it first turns into a bitch and then disappears.[6]

Many accounts have been given of a creature called the "Fellow Traveller" (*synodoiporo*) who joins travellers along a road, but disappears into thin air when the road passes a church.[7]

Other *xotika* are evident for what they are by their constant shape-shifting. Thus when one young man was returning home at night he saw a creature that resembled a hedgehog in front of him, but it kept changing size. Luckily he lit a cigarette and said a prayer, and since both light and prayer were deterrents to the *xotika*, he survived.[8] The neighbourhood of Limnes and Prosymna, in the Argolid, for example, was famous for the frequency with which people see animals which appear out of nowhere and change their shape.[9]

Some spirits are known only by the sounds they make. For example, Mount Ekato, near Sochos in Chalcidice, echoed at night to "shrill laughter, loud wailing, and other weird sounds" which did not proceed from any mortal lungs.[10]

The word *telonia* was used to describe a wide variety of unusual appearances of light in the atmosphere, including comets and shooting stars. But the most feared manifestation of the *telonia* was the phenomenon of Saint Elmo's fire: the light which flickers around the mastheads of ships during storms. It was held to portend an attack by malevolent aerial powers. Accordingly, many measures were taken to drive it away, including invocation of the saints, spells against demons, the firing of guns, and driving a black-handled knife into the mast.[11]

Bent witnessed the return to Kimolos of a young sailor who had lost his reason on a sea voyage. As his ship had rounded Cape Malea a terrible storm had arisen, and a light, called the *telonia* had appeared at the masthead. The sailor's condition was said to be the result. He was taken to the church of Saint Katharina, where they prayed over him for him to recover his wits.[12]

In Athens it was believed that the *telonia*, like the *kallikantzaroi*, infested the seas for the twelve days of Christmas, so that ships should be kept in harbour during this period, setting out only after the blessing of the waters on *Theophania* (Epiphany).[13]

Spirits of the air were blamed for medical problems in some areas. This was true of the once malarial marshes of the Stryma in Macedonia.[14]

In the same region, women who are belated on the road and seized with sudden terror, resulting in temporary loss of speech, moping madness, or malignant ague, and said to be under attack from an *aeriko,* or spirit of the air. Recourse was immediately had to some renowned dervish or Mohammedan religious minister of the neighbourhood, who would pretend to trace the evil to its source, and to discover the exact spot on the road where the attack occurred. That place is sprinkled with boiled grape-juice, on three consecutive nights, so that the temper of the spirit responsible for the problem might be sweetened.[15]

Anomalous auditory phenomena are also attributed to *aerika*. Mount Ekato, near Sochos, in the Chalkidic peninsula, echoes night and day to shrill laughter, loud wailing, and other noises which do not come from mortal sources.[16]

The people of Kollines on "Kupho Voini" in Arcadia fear a spirit called Panagitsa, which takes the form of an invisible bird which imitates various sounds and calls to lure people over a precipice.[17]

The Armenides appear in flashes of light. The name means "Armenian". It is thought that Armenians were unpopular because they were thought to collaborate with the Turks.[18]

Such lights were said to lure people to their deaths. This sounds like good advice to travellers in rough country not to head straight and incautiously towards a distant light, as there might be many dangers hidden in the darkness in between the traveller and the light.

The village of Vythos, near Kozani, was troubled by a haunting in 1952. In the house of Stavroula, the widow of Apostolos Magianni and her three daughters, loud noises were heard from the basement, and the furniture began to move about by itself. The terrified women passed three sleepless nights together around the stove. This did not protect them, for the firewood was moved, threatening the house with being burned down. The president of the community sent for Mr. Tanagras, of the Society for Psychical Research. They sent a team of seven men to investigate these phenomena. These informed the public that they had heard sounds and seen objects moving of their own accord. One night, a local priest, Geronikolas, stayed there and said that during the night a door had opened, and that on the threshold he saw the shadow of an old woman who threw an apple from the family store at him. Undeterred, he addressed the phantom: "Why have you returned to us at this time from the other world?" Startled, she put out the oil lamp with which the room was illuminated, closed the door noisily and disappeared. The same old woman approached another person in the house, observing that the room beside the one they were in she had heard a noise.

Other villagers told that the family had in the house a sheepdog on the previous Saturday. At about midnight it began a woeful howling, and continued until the morning. It was found, sweating and breathing with difficulty in a corner of one of the rooms of the house. One night, when the family and neighbours were praying before the icons, the icon of the

Crucified left its place, described a circle in the air and then stood up perpendicularly by itself on the ground. Terrified, everyone fled to a neighbour's house, where they all remained locked in for the rest of the night. In the morning, they had another surprise. In front of the flying icon were placed crosswise two axes which had been in the family store. One of those who returned fell over a small stool which had been mysteriously placed in the way.

A newspaper reporter who visited the family was told that one night there was a loud sound, and everyone gathered together to see what would happen. These included a relative, Amalia Aragia, who shouted that if the ghost did not go away, she would go to the church to get her sent away. After that everything went quiet and there was no more trouble. But as they were talking, he noticed that the stone covering of the vessel that the family was using to boil chestnuts on the fire was lifting up very slowly. But he did not hear the characteristic sound of water hissing when it boiled. Besides, he did not believe that the water in the pot was boiling. Moreover, the lid resumed the exact place that it had occupied before it had moved.[19]

Late one night in the country town of Yiannitsa in 1950, Sideris Gialamoudis and his family were alarmed to hear loud, hollow-sounding noises coming from the basement of their house. When they looked outside, they saw what appeared to be a number of human shapes or shadows moving around outside. The terrified family rushed out into the road, calling for help from their neighbours. On the next night, many of these volunteered to stay with them during the night. Suddenly, at midnight, the stove was opened by some unknown power, and small fires scattered over the floor. Many of these were certain that they had seen a shadow approach the stove just before it was opened. These were hardy villagers, and they decided to adopt the methods they would use to hunt wolves to identify the *phantasmata*. The next night they covered the floor of the basement with ashes, so as to reveal the footprints of any intruders, and surrounded the house with an "iron ring" of armed townspeople. Strange noises were heard over a wide radius, and something moved the furniture and other things about inside the house. In the morning the villagers examined the layer of ashes they had laid down, and found many footprints, but all seemed to be of two-footed goats, sheep and pigs, and no one had seen anything like that. For the sake of the health of the family, it was considered necessary for them to build another house, and move into it. In the meantime, several skeletons were dug up with helmets and breastplates in the neighbourhood. The haunting had almost been forgotten by most people, when new loud noises were heard all over the neighbourhood. They began to dig all over the village to excavate skeletons, which they had come to believe were remains of an ancient battle. They believed that it was from them that the hauntings came.[20]

All over Greece the stillness of nature at high noon in summer was dreaded as a dangerous hour, and the "Noonday Demon" was feared. In the Mani he was known as Makrynas "The Faraway One". He would appear to women in lonely places at the haunted hour, causing them to flee in panic. The Midnight spirit lay in wait for anyone returning home late. The Bad Hour, or Dangerous Hour, was held responsible for much sickness and death, and sometimes appeared as a small black dog, although it might take many other forms, e.g. a shadow, donkey or baby.[21]

Stone throwing spirits seem to be common. Pashely recorded in Crete: "My hostess here, at Annapolis, was once traversing the mountains, accompanied by one of her daughters, and, when about three miles from the village of Muri, they heard sounds as of voices singing, but it was impossible to distinguish what were the words uttered. The demon, for such she supposed the unseen object of her alarm to be, then began to throw stones, which fell both before and behind them. Although she saw him not, yet she immediately pronounced aloud some holy texts, which are a never failing charm against any common demon. When she found that the evil spirit continued to sing, and to cast stones at them, she knew that it must he a Katakhanas; and, therefore, crossing herself, and calling on the Holy Mother of God, she immediately repeated: "In the beginning was the Word, and the Word was with God, and the Word was God." This sentence she pronounced thrice, but it was all in vain: the Katakhanas kept rolling down the stones as before, She next repeated a part of the Greek ritual, which produced no better effect: the Katakhanas continued to persecute and terrify her. At length, on seeing two women, as she approached the village, she summoned courage enough to address him in a bolder strain', and, on her doing so, he ceased to molest her."[22]

Mysterious lights wandering about the countryside after darkness falls have long haunted certain areas. They rise in the same places, follow the same routes and disappear in the same places, year after year. Such lights are seen at Tatoi, outside Athens,[23] and the area around the chapel of Saint George and the archaeological site at Vraona, also in Attica.[24]

Such a wandering light in the village of Kollines, in Arcadia, emerges from the church of Saint Dimitrios, goes to the village cemetery, descends into a ravine, and disappears near a shrine.[25] On the road between Serres and Zichnis is a small bridge. Travellers approaching from a distance see a light on the bridge. As they approach, however, it disappears, and an eerie form seems to walk silently on the bridge in the shadows.[26] On Tinos such lights are said only to disappear with the barking of a dog or the screaming of a pig.[27]

In 1935 a light rose out of the cemetery of Palaiokastro, Gortynia, one night, and flew through the air, to the consternation of many people sitting outside the village shop, who sat watching it go by.[28]

These lights do not always wander. In Skoulikadiko in Zakynthos they talk of a mill which the villagers had to work in late in the evenings, which would be lit up by an intense ghostly light. In Karytainas they see a light in a place where a chapel once stood.[29]

When such lights appear in the sky, they may perhaps be thought of in terms of the more general UFOs which are reported worldwide. Among these would be included the appearances of moving lights over Thessaloniki and the Thermaic Gulf during the latter half of the twentieth century.[30] During the autumn of 1992, the Saronic Gulf in the area of Porto Heli and Spetses was troubled by repeated sightings of luminous discs in the sky.[31]

[1] Abbott 251-2

[2] e.g. Νουάρου 247.

[3] Βαού.

[4] Durrell 40-1.

[5] Abbott 252.

[6] Πολίτης 2:335-6.

[7] Θεοδοσιάδης 81.

[8] Blum & Blum 108.

[9] Τσικλίδης (2) 1:251.

[10] Abbott 250.

[11] Lawson 286.

[12] Bent 24.

[13] Lawson 285.

[14] Abbott 224.

[15] Abbott 225.

[16] Abbott 250.

[17] Τσικλίδης (2) 2:86.

[18] Stewart 171.

[19] Σερέφας 89-93.

[20] Σερεφάς 89-93.

[21] Blum & Blum 104.

[22] Pashley 2:219.

[23] Τσικλίδης (1) 2:45.

[24] Τσικλίδης (1) 1:105.

[25] Τσικλίδης (2) 1:

[26] Αυλίδου, 133.

[27] Καναράκης, 401.

[28] Τσικλίδης (2) 2:204.

[29] Τσικλίδης (2) 2:203.

[30] Σερεφάς 122-31.

[31] Νικολούλη.

Powers of Evil

As we have had ample evidence to see, *xotika* were frequently malign and dangerous. Such spirits were frequently called "demons." Some places were notorious meeting places of demons. They were inclined to lay tables at crossroads, and if people should walk by and accidentally step on the table, they would attack, driving their victims insane or bewitching them.[1] The ravines of Davia on Zakynthos were so haunted by demons that no one dared go there at night alone. In the village of Bonato they lurked in the shadows, and disappeared into the air at the stroke of midnight. The villagers erected a large column with an image of the *Panayia*[2] on it to discourage them.[3] In Lagana, on the same island, there is a spring called Vrontonero, which made a moaning sound. There tall, slender demons with long narrow heads and large horns, goats' feet and tails, gathered at night.[4] Demons seem to have held the upper hand on Kefallonia. There are some fathomless holes in the ground near

Sami where once the people built churches. The buildings sank in to the ground, and those places became gathering places for demons.[5]

Churches were sometimes built near places haunted by demons in an effort to hold them in check, such as the little church of Saint Nicholas at Kataphyki, in the Argolid, which was, according to tradition, built in the cave for precisely that reason. It was supposed to have been successful, in that afterwards, the demons no longer troubled anyone any more.[6]

In Crete it was believed that babies who died before being baptized became little demons covered in black feathers. Those who pass the places where they are buried after dark sometimes heard strange noises, and saw sparks of light coming from out of the earth. They flew about after dark and specialized in throwing stones at travellers.[7]

The people of the island of Alonnisos, in the Northern Sporades, were, until recently, particularly fearful of demons, which were frequently seen by the islanders: "On Alonnisos people see devils as frequently as on other islands they see tourists." They would even enter the churches and follow boats at sea. Certain places in the village were notoriously gathering places for the creatures, and would be avoided after darkness fell.[8]

The hole of Katafikios, near Ermioni, was believed to be an entrance to Hades, and was haunted by demons, which issued out at night and tormented the neighbourhood. A chapel was erected there dedicated to Saint Nicholas, and from that time onward, the problem ceased.[9]

During the nineteenth century, blustery winds on Santorini were popularly attributed to demons rushing about hither and thither.[10]

A friend of Lawrence Durrell was holidaying on Santorini near Thira when the peasants called her to see a "devil" hiding in an olive tree playing on his pipes. She could not see anything, but four other people claimed to have spotted him; although she could hear faint music and the clicking of hoofs. Then he jumped down and everyone fled screaming.[11]

The sharp division of all paranormal beings into good and evil was foreign to Greek thought, as was that dichotomy itself. The "Devil" was probably a Persian concept which reached Greece in Christianity, via Judaism, and was foreign to Greece before the advent of Christianity. Greek converts seem to have assimilated "the devil and his angels" by identifying them with Pan and the satyrs. Certainly Pan and the satyrs are clearly evident in ecclesiastical portrayals of devils with goats' horns and hoofs, general hairiness and large phalli. None of these things are characteristics of Satan or the devils in the New Testament.

When the scriptural teaching and doctrines and traditions of the Church were assimilated by the population, it established that there were two different sets of creatures: the Devil and his demons (required by Orthodoxy) and the various *exotika* (existing superstitions), side by side. Over the centuries the two have become confused to some extent.[12]

In many places, the distinction between the two hardly exists today. For example, in the Pindus Mountains of northern Greece, both the devil and the *exotika* may be heard playing musical instruments in riverbeds.

Some people, in telling a story about *xotika,* may purposely change its name or species to that of "devil" in order to escape the charge of superstition. For others, the *xotika* have simply become devils. They may be referred to as *diavoloi* or *satanades*. The pagan world-view has for them become entirely assimilated into the official Orthodox cosmology. Thus someone from Leros could say: "The nereids, according to our grandfathers and grandmothers, are the annoyance sent by an enemy. That is, they are the force of the Devil."[13]

When this assimilation had reached a certain level, the belief arose that the *xotika* deliberately persecuted the clergy and monks. Also, people would ascribe to devils acts which were elsewhere ascribed to *xotika*. Thus a woman in the lowland village of Tripodes, on Naxos, told Charles Stewart: "I was unchurched and I got up one night to pee in the courtyard of our house. It was around midnight. The Devil followed me back into the house. I caught sight of him. He had a huge head and lots of black hair. His power was so great, however, that I couldn't speak to warn my husband who was sleeping in the bed with the child. He tried to get me to come to an outlying area of the village....

To show his power over me he ordered me to tear up a sheet, which I did, ripping it into three pieces. But his power was not absolute and I was able to spring to the cabinet and pick up a small bottle of holy water. When he saw what I had in my hand he tried to hide himself under the bed. I threw some of the water under there and then out came a cloud of black smoke that blew out the door.

That was an experience of fifty years ago, but I'll never forget it."

Stewart points out that although this story was associated in the woman's mind with the Devil, on other parts of the island it would have been attributed to a *gello* or *stringla*.[14]

The Devil became, for many Greeks, a fearful presence. He was rarely named, save indirectly, or under some euphemistic title, such as "the wanderer", "the good man", the Black One," or the Unmentionable One."[15]

Sometimes he was portrayed as performing his biblical function of tempter. He was said to break up marriages, often disguising himself as a friend in order to do so.[16] The devil could take many guises in which to do evil: "Old Mrs. Kerimis remembers the time when she took the sheep out to pasture: 'I was sitting on the side of the hill watching the flock, and from out of nowhere my husband appeared and began beating me with a stick. I screamed and begged him to stop, but he didn't. My real husband came and found me and took me to the priest. When I woke up he was praying over me to drive out the Devil. I know it was real because when my husband found me I was cut and bruised. I had black and blue marks all over my body for almost two weeks."[17]

Yet the devil never entirely lost his original character as a *xotiko*. Sometimes he was manifested to the eye in the form of an animal, a black horse or a black ass. The Mainotes, in whose land is the famous cave of Taenaron, one of the entrances to the Underworld, preserve the tradition of a black dog, that issues from its recesses and runs about the earth, an unconscious reminiscence perhaps of Cerberus. More commonly it is the form of a goat which the demonic power assumes; and in Mani, again, there is a folk-song which tells how one who was on his way to avenge an insult by shooting his enemy invoked the devil's aid, addressing a goat which he heard bleating by the name of Satan.[18]

In many parts of Greece there was real fear of the half-human, half-animal "limping demon", sometimes known as "Koutsogianni" (Lame John), a creature of hideous exterior, with the legs of a goat, with a hairy face, a long bearded, and a horned head which butted with terrible effect, and generally appeared in company with the *Kallikantsari*. On account of his lameness he always lagged behind, but he was the most dreaded, the most relentless and the most terrible of all the evil spirits, combining the visible characteristics of Hephaistos and Pan with the moral and theological evil of the Christian devil.[19] His lameness was explained in a very widespread story. The devil tried to create a man, but brought into being a wolf instead by mistake. The wolf, on coming alive, attacked the devil and chewed its creator's foot.[20]

There grew up a tendency to attribute all evil the devil, and to regard and all malignant spirits as devils, his agents, in areas, and among sections of the population, where the cosmology of the inhabitants was most deeply affected by Christianity.

This was evident in many of the testimonies made to Scott G. McNall in rural Attica in the late nineteen sixties.

Thus one man reported:

"Suddenly, my daughter could not move one of her legs. She got up one morning and fell to the floor. I knew it must be the Devil's doing so I went to Mrs. Psilos, who knows about these things. She said that I needed a hair as long as my child. I brought it to her, and she went inside but she would not let me follow. I saw her drop it in a basin of water. Soon she returned and told me that my child was not afflicted by the Devil. But she did not get well. I went to the priest, who took my daughter behind the church, and then brought her back to me. He said that I was to take her home on the donkey and as soon as I lifted her down at home she would be able to walk. She did."[21]

A soldier in northern Greece was out in the countryside one very dark night and heard a sheep or goat bell in the distance and saw a light. He went towards it. Suddenly he was overwhelmed with the feeling that something was wrong, and stopped abruptly. Peering into the blackness, he saw that he was on the edge of a cliff. With one more step he would have plunged to his death. He immediately attributed the noise and the light to the Devil.[22]

People seemed to "just know" that what confronted them on some particular occasion was "the Devil." An Attic villager said: "Once I had to leave the house at three in the morning to take our vegetables to the market in Kapandriton. As I was walking across the fields I heard a cock crowing. I knew something was wrong, because cocks do not crow at that time of night. Finally I saw it. It was riding on the back of a donkey, with the reins in its beak. It crossed in front of me, and disappeared over the hill. I knew it was the Devil."[23]

Other sightings of *xotika* in the neighbourhood were said to be "devils." Thus a tall shadow of a black-robed priest about two metres high seen on the road near Erythra, in Attica, was called the "devil," and on the next night seen and exorcised by two priests.[24] Similarly, a small human-shaped creature which haunted a cave on Mount Kithaeron was also described by local people as a devil.[25]

Demon possession is recognised by the Church, which, of course, regards the demons as either Satan or his agents. Sometimes the priests are called upon to exorcise such people. One priest related to Scott McNall:

"She was very weak, this woman. She had low morals. The Devil usually possesses weak people. She would tremble and fall into a coma and then the Devil would speak through her mouth. She said that she would destroy God and all of his sheep, and cursed the priesthood. While she shouted I pretended not to hear her and continued to say prayers. The Devil left and entered her body three times. Finally, on the fourth try, I drove the Devil from her body. This woman has not been possessed now for over twenty years."[26]

Some monasteries or churches specialise in exorcism of demons and the devil, such as the monastery of SS Cyprian and Justina at Phyle (Hasia) outside Athens, and the Church of the Saviour at Spata, near the International Airport.

As part of the same synthesis, vampirism sometimes came to be understood as demon-possession of the corpse. An informant told Lee: "The *vrykolakas* is the devil";[27] but this tendency can be traced back as far as the Catholic churchman, Leo Allatius.[28] The vampire was inhabited by an evil spirit which had displaced the dead soul, which explained its more than usual ferocity. A Cretan abbot explained this as follows:

" . . . after the separation of the soul from the body there enters into the latter an evil spirit, which takes the place of the soul and assumes the shape of the dead man and so is transformed into a *vrykolakas* or man-demon.

'In this guise it keeps the body as its dwelling-place and preserves it from corruption, and it runs swift as lightning wherever it lists, and causes men great alarms at night and strikes all with panic. And the trouble is that it does not remain solitary, but makes everyone, who dies while it is about, like to itself, so that in a short space of time it gets together a large and dangerous train of followers . . .

'This monster, as time goes on, becomes more and more audacious and bloodthirsty, so that it is able completely to devastate whole villages."[29]

It is not within the remit of this book to consider in detail Greek witches, often considered to be servants of the Devil. However, given the indefiniteness of the boundaries of the various categories of *xotika* recognised by the Greek imagination, it is hardly surprising that in this tradition witches sometimes appear as more than purely human.

The status of the traditional witch, or wise woman, was described thus by a visitor to Crete during the 1880s:

"They adore the old hag of their community, who has got a sound reputation as a seer, wise woman, healer, etc. She it is that they fly to when any actual ills assail them. The priest is very well as a mere ritual-monger; otherwise he has to find his level among them as best he may, on the strength of his particular endowments as a layman. And, to complete the circuit of ancient error which has these people in its thrall, the very priest himself has as much regard for the wise woman of the village as any other of the villagers have. I was even told of a worthy ecclesiastic who hastened miles across the mountains to procure a charm from one of these old and ugly dames, that he might hang it round the neck of his daughter, who was sick."[30]

The home of witchcraft in ancient Greece was Thessally,[31] but in modern Greece, many places were famous for their witches, including the town of Megara and the island of Salamis. The witches of Nymphaiou, Florina, were once famous for standing naked at midnight on the covers of springs to make their magic.[32]

The village of Lefkes, on Paros, enjoyed the reputation of having many witches, old men and women of above a hundred years of age, who haunted the caves on the mountainside. They could turn into birds at will, and some had the heads of women and the bodies of birds.[33] They were also cannibals, although for choice they would always prefer the flesh of unbaptized babies.[34]

[1] e.g. Πολίτης 1:390.

[2] The Virgin Mary

[3] Θεοδοσιάδης (3) 470.

[4] Θεοδοσιάδης, 82.

[5] Θεοδοσιάδης (3) 478.

[6] Σεραφείμ 384.

[7] Θεοδοσιάδης 80.

[8] Carroll 159-60.

[9] Τσικλίδης (2) 1:263.

[10] Bent 71.

[11] Durrell 114.

[12] Πολίτης 2:234-5.

[13] Quoted in Stewart 275.

[14] Stewart 99-100.

[15] Rodd 202.

[16] Blum & Blum 99.

[17] Mcnall 70.
[18] Edwards 357-8.
[19] Halliday 54-5.
[20] Πολίτης 1:381.
[21] NcNall 70.
[22] Stewart 104.
[23] Mcnall 69.
[24] Τσικλίδης (1) 2:122.
[25] Τσικλίδης (1) 2.123.
[26] McNall 68.
[27] Lee.
[28] Rodd 192.
[29] Quoted in Lawson 372-3.
[30] Edwards 357-8.
[31] Halliday 54-5.
[32] Αυλίδος 136.
[33] Moussa 72.
[34] Bent 187.

The Guardians

The Christian saints would seem to belong to quite a different environment and cultural *milieu* from the *xotika*, and to have no connection whatever with folklore. Yet that this is not so can be seen on many counts.

If we consider the number of churches dedicated to each of the saints the number of children named after them, and the importance of their festivals, and compare this with their importance in the Gospels or in the history of the Church, it is clear that certain saints enjoy a popularity which can in no way be explained by their importance in Christianity.

Out of all the many Old Testament figures commemorated in the services of the Orthodox Church, only one, the prophet Elijah, has a feast day of national importance (*Profitis Ilias*), gives his name to many boys, and has countless churches and chapels dedicated in his honour across the country. When we notice that virtually all the churches and chapels dedicated to him are on mountain peaks or hilltops, it becomes clear that there must be a connection between that particular saint and the sites chosen for his chapels. In the Old Testament story, Elijah built an altar on Mount Carmel and offered sacrifice there in contest with the prophets of Baal, bringing to an end a deadly drought.[1] Later, he was taken up into heaven in a whirlwind.[2] In ancient times, hilltop shrines in Greece were often dedicated to Zeus, to whom people prayed for rain. The Church authorities clearly used him as a Christian interpretation of the ongoing cult of Zeus the rain-giver on hilltops. Other hilltop shrines were dedicated to Helios, or Apollo as the sun. The coincidence of the name was also used to give a Christian interpretation to these hilltop shrines. The thinness of the new identification is evident from the fact that traditional bonfires are still lit on hilltops on his feast day,[3] and until recently the colour of the smoke of the fires would be used to make predictions about the future.[4]

The extremely popular saints George, Demetrios and Nicholas are other obvious examples of saints whose ubiquitous popularity can have little to do with their historical stature. George and Demetrios were Roman soldiers, George came from Cappadocia, in what is now Turkey, and Demetrios from Thessaloniki. Both were martyred, like many others, in the persecution under the emperor Diocletian. The first two are portrayed as archetypal "holy warriors," and inherited the ancient holy places dedicated to heroes, such as Herakles or Theseus. Nicholas was an early fourth century archbishop of Lycia, also in present-day Turkey. Nicholas became protector of all who travel by sea, and his stern bearded face replaced that of Poseidon.

Other saints, such as Marina and Paraskevi, have a similarly inexplicable popularity. The identification of ancient gods with modern saints is clear in some cases by name. Demeter has become Saint Dimitros, and Artemis Saint Artemidos. It seems likely that early Greek Christians treated saints by analogy with heroes: men who had become like gods, worthy recipients of the homage of a cult. This is evident in some of the popular stories about the saints, such as the following, which was told just before the First World War by a peasant on Euboea.

Saint Dionysios, on his way to Naxos, saw a small plant which excited his wonder. He dug it up, and because the sun was hot sought shelter for it. Looking about he saw the bone of a bird's leg and he placed the plant in it to keep it safe, but the plant grew and grew, and looking about for a larger covering he came upon the leg-bone of a lion. Unable to detach the bird's bone he placed the whole inside the lion's bone. But again it grew and grew and, as he looked about, he came upon the leg-bone of an ass and placed the whole thing in that. So he came to Naxos and, when he planted the first vine, for this little plant was the first vine, he could not detach it from its coverings, so he buried the whole lot together. Then the vine grew grapes and men made wine, and drank of it for the first time! At first when they drank they sang like birds; then, continuing, they grew strong like lions; but continuing thus, they last of all became as foolish as asses.[5]

Clearly, this "Saint Dionysios" is the none other than the vine-wreathed god, Dionysos.

A rather mercenary attitude is adopted towards the saints, illustrated by two sayings from Aperianthos, in Naxos: "Whichever saint does not work wonders is not honoured," and "Even the saints need threatening."[6] That the mercenary nature of the relationship works both ways can be shown by a story from the same island reported by Stewart. At some period during the latter half of the nineteenth century, a shepherd was grazing his flocks on Mount Fanari when he slipped over a cliff. As he was falling, he managed to cry out to the Panayia to save him, and promise that if she did so, he would build a chapel on the spot. It was as though a hand had grabbed him, and he fell softly, as though on to feathers. Afterwards, he built the chapel of Phanariotissa.[7] The saints are resorted to in sickness, as is evidenced by the *tamata* hung before their icons, and may work miracles of healing. A visit to many churches even in Athens will show that this belief is still widespread, for many icons of powerful saints, or powerful icons, have rows of *tamata* hanging before them.

Apart from an inclination towards benevolence, the behaviour attributed to the saints sometimes resembles nothing so much as a *xotika*.

In 1942 Saint Paraskevi was believed by many to have visited the island of Poros. She travelled about as a wandering woman begging alms, and blessing all who gave to her. One day she left for Methona as a passenger in a launch. Half way there, the captain began to have trouble with the motor and blasphemed. The outraged saint revealed herself by promptly making the sign of the cross, rising into the air, and flying across to Methona. She was later observed begging in that village. News of her presence spread far and wide, and became a major topic of conversation throughout the region.[8]

Animal features are characteristic of *xotika*, but also of at least one saint. In Christian popular tradition, Saint Christopher was a giant who

159

carried travellers across a river, and according to the well-known story, one day he carried across a child who turned out to be Christ in disguise as a child. Old traditions of the life of the saint, even in the Western Church, however, contain a curious detail, according to which "he was of the race of mankind who are half hound." He came "from the nation where men have the head of a dog and from the country where men devour each other," and that he "had the head of a hound, and his locks were extremely long, and his eyes shone as bright as the morning star, and his teeth were as sharp as a boar's tusks." This saint's cult is centred on the island of Tilos. There the story was that he was so handsome that his admirers would not allow him to follow the path to sainthood he had chosen, so God helped him out by substituting his head for that of a dog, so that they would leave him alone. A seventeenth century icon from there, now in the Byzantine Museum, Athens, depicts the result of this drastic solution. The saint wears sacerdotal vestments, bears a cross, and has a halo, but the last surrounds the head of a dog. Clearly, this is not the simple patron saint of travellers.[9] Other icons of the saint with the head of a dog have been found in Anatolia and Russia.

There is a strange chapel at Alepochori, near Lampi, in Thrace, about eight kilometres from the Bulgarian border, mostly buried beneath the ground, where the faces of the saints on the icons are those of animals.[10]

Dog-headed devils appear in folk tales.[11] In Messenia there are stories of a dog-headed people who had their own village, Vizie, near Palaiogoula of Sparta. They stole girls from nearby villages and made war on their neighbours.[12]

Near the port of Plakas, Leonidou, on the road to Poulithra is a hill called Viglas, believed once to have been inhabited by a race of man-eating beings with the heads of dogs and the bodies of men. At the same time, on the nearby mountain of Ayios Athanasios there was a tribe of ordinary humans. Both would draw water from Kefalovruso, which is in a *rema* in the village. Friction between the two tribes arose because one day a girl from Ayios Athanasios went to the spring to get water, and was taken by the dog-headed tribe. After some time, the girl's brother went looking for her. The dog-headed people strangled him, put him in a cauldron and boiled him, in order to eat him. When his sister found out what had happened, she committed suicide. Another version of the end of the story says that the dog-headed people kidnapped the girl and cooked her. Then they invited the people of Ayios Athanasios to the feast. During the meal, her family recognised what they were eating because of a ring which was still on her hand. According to George

Balanos, graves containing bodies of tall people with unusually large canine teeth have been excavated in the area which was supposedly inhabited by the dog-headed people in this story.[13]

Some stories show that it is not always clear in the folk mind if an event is to be ascribed to a saint or a *xotiko*.

Near Davia, in the neighbourhood of Mainolo, in Arcadia, lived a priest. He had a haystack near a threshing floor, and one day took his horse to thresh, even though it was the feast of Ayia Marina. In the middle of the day, when everyone else was resting, the priest was still working hard. At that time a beautiful women with golden hair dressed in white came up to him, greeted him, and asked him what he was doing on such a day. Because he was too busy, he merely told her that he did not need to justify himself to her. At that, there was a booming sound and an earthquake hit the area. When the inhabitants rushed out of their houses, the threshing floor, the horse and the priest had all disappeared, and where they had been was a new sink hole, or *katavothra*. Some said that the woman was Ayia Marina herself, who had come to punish the priest for breaking the peace of her feast day. But others said it was a nereid, sent by the Lady, because at that time of day they were accustomed to eat, and he was disturbing their peace.[14]

Menelaos Tsiklidis was told a story by an inhabitant of Stemnitsa about a relative who was driving his car very fast on the road from Dimitsana to Stemnitsa and had reached the monastery of Saint John the Forerunner, when he saw standing in the middle of the road ahead of him a tall figure wearing a shepherd's cloak and hood. Naturally he braked, in order not to run the man down, and stopped to speak to him. But when he started to open the car door, he realised that there was no face inside the hood, he quickly closed it and drove away. Although not a religious man, the motorist's interpretation of his experience was that it was Saint John who had appeared to him to prevent him from killing himself by driving too fast.[15]

Sometimes, the saint is little more than a *xotiko* made "respectable." Abbott observes: "Many springs in Macedonia are known and venerated as sacred waters dedicated to Saint Paraskevi . . . The water of such springs is regarded as efficacious against diseases, especially eye-complaints. They are generally enclosed within a stone parapet, and sometimes roofed in, as a protection from accidental pollution."[16] Saint Paraskevi has clearly inherited the healing waters of the nymphs. Near Kalamata, the Virgin Mary, the *Panayia,* is actually said to have appeared in the water of a well above Pepandi Square, although one had to be a Christian to see her.[17]

Sometimes the saints take on the character of guardians of a particular community, like benevolent spirits of place.

The churches of Dimitsana, in Arcadia, each had their own spirit, which people would occasionally hear calling during the night.[18] The spirit of Ayios Yeorgios, Stemnitsa, was most splendid sight. It was a horse with golden shoes and a silver saddle, reins and bridle. Its rider, identified as Saint George, carried in his hand a golden spear.[19] Here Saint George appears to have become the *genius loci*.

Although of considerable repute in ancient times, the modern town of Megara is usually bypassed by Greeks and tourists alike on the fast road between Athens and the Isthmus of Corinth. In popular belief today, the town lies under the special protection of ten supernatural guardians, the Ten Holy Martyrs of Megara. They appear when they are needed, although usually at night, and then disappear into the darkness. On occasions of special danger to the people of the town, they have, however, manifested themselves in broad daylight. They took part in the struggle of the Megariotes against the Turks in the War of Independence, and assisted them during the German Occupation.

Many stories are told about their oversight of the town, and of their aid to the inhabitants during the German-Italian Occupation (1941-44). It was said that whenever German bombers approached Megara, dense cloud cover would shroud the city, so that the crews would be unable to target the town to drop their bombs. This would happen even during periods of otherwise fine weather. The airmen would take off in cloudless skies, but as they approached the town, clouds would invariably form again.

Individuals frequently believe themselves have benefited from the intervention of the Holy Ten, no less than the community as a whole, and in Megara two large churches are being built in commemoration of their many miracles.[20]

Sailors pray to the Virgin, as well as Saint Nicholas, for safety at sea. There are many stories of how sailors in danger turned to the Virgin for aid. In the sixteenth century icon from Perivoli, Mytilene, the figures of the *Panayia* and *Gorgona* are combined. Novelist Stratis Myrivilis used this perfect combination of the two heritages of Modern Greece, pagan and Christian, in his *Mermaid Madonna (I Panagia I Gorgona):*

"Her head is rendered in the familiar, conventional Byzantine style: dark-complexioned face, sensitively drawn, with an expression of reserve, a rounded chin, almond eyes, and a small mouth. A purple pallium surrounds the upper part of her body and veils her head down to her eyebrows. There is also the golden halo, as in all icons. Her eyes are extraordinarily wide and green in colour. But from the waist down, she is a fish with blue scales; and in one hand she holds a ship and in the other a trident like that of the ancient sea god Poseidon.

When the fishermen and villagers first saw this painting, they stood in wonder before it, but it did not seem odd to them. The women said their prayers to it and offered it incense as they did to the other icons.

It was called the Mermaid Madonna, as it is to this day, and from it, the chapel and the port took their names. No one stopped to reflect that, on the day this Madonna was conceived in the mind of the old hermit, there sprang as from the head of Zeus, and established herself on this unique rock near an Aegean island, a new Greek divinity, who in a miraculous manner united all the epochs and all the meaning of the race - a race that struggles with the elements and tempests of the world, on land and sea, with the ploughshare and the keel, always subject to a warlike divinity, female and virgin.

The villagers, the fishermen, the skippers and passing sea-captains regarded the Mermaid Madonna without surprise, for she already resided in their souls, whence Captain Lias had dived and brought her up, and thus they had known her long before he gave her to them on the chapel wall."[21]

[1] I *Kings* 18.

[2] II *Kings* 2.

[3] Tomkinson (4) 104.

[4] Megas 142.

[5] Βούρνας και Γαρίδη 165.

[6] Stewart 81.

[7] Stewart 81.

[8] Gray.

[9] Stewart 155.

[10] Στάμκος 24.

[11] e.g. Πολίτης 1:397.

[12] Θεοδοσιάδης (1) 365.

[13] Τσικλίδης (2) 2:293-4.

[14] Πολίτη, 1. 33.

[15] Τσικλίδης (2) 2:197.

[16] Abbott, 244.

[17] Stewart, 157.

[18] Πολίτης 1:292-3.

[19] Τσικλίδης (2) 2:196

[20] Τσικλίδης (1) 2:88-90.

[21] Myrivilis 9-10.

The Departure of the *Exotika*

The winter of 1923-24 was a difficult one throughout Greece. The unfortunate refugees from Asia Minor were facing their first winter in the country, often without proper homes, heating, clothes or food. For this reason, the streets of Thessaloniki were not as animated as usual after darkness fell.

Then the story spread across the city that an apparition had been seen stalking the streets in the district of Kamara after dark. It moved along the narrow road now called Elenis Svoronou, and disappeared into the wall of the Protestant cemetery. Most apprehensive were those who had to use this road to get to and from the Municipal Hospital of Saint Demetrios.

As the story spread, the churches became crowded in the mornings by people offering prayers for the exorcism of the spirit from the city. Many took good care to rush home before darkness fell and bolted themselves securely in their homes. They lit lamps and candles before their icons, and burned incense. They placed crosses on the insides of their doors and windows, and also vessels of water, the last an old spell, to banish the spirit to the mountains.

In the *taverna* of Lekka, in the district of Kamara, all the talk was of the phantom, until two men who had drunk rather too much silenced everyone by publicly resolving to go out to the spot and wait to see what passed by. Some of those present tried to dissuade them; others applauded their design, but when they saw that they were genuinely intent upon going, made the sign of the cross on their foreheads to protect them from the apparition.

Only when the two emerged into the cold night outside the *taverna* did the possible consequences of their rash resolution begin to dawn upon them. As they sobered up, they realised that if they backed out, their friends, the other patrons of the *taverna*, and the entire neighbourhood, would henceforward regard them as empty boasters and cowards.

They did not go straight to the spot which was supposed to be haunted, but took a circuitous route to get to the entrance of the Municipal Hospital on the other side, for there was a single gas lamp, which threw a little light into the general gloom of the street. From that side they ventured into the darkness, and waited beside the wall of the cemetery. Above their heads the cypresses whispered in the wind, and the owls hooted. After what seemed an eternity, they heard midnight chime, and decided with relief that nothing was going to happen, and that they might go home without having compromised their reputations.

At that moment one of them spotted a strange winged form quickly approaching them in the darkness. Feeling that he was about to faint with fear, he nudged his companion. When he, in his turn, saw what was drawing near, he simply froze, without being able to move a muscle.

It was only when it was quite close that they realised that the strange sounds they had begun to hear were the words of a popular song. It was sung in the cinema at that time during the intermission, the words being displayed on a board above the screen. The "apparition," wearing a cloak, passed them by cheerily and hopped over a breach in the wall of the cemetery, crossed to another low wall between the cemetery and the hospital, stepped over it, and disappeared inside.

The two heroes returned directly to the *taverna*, where fears for their safety had grown with the length of their absence, to the point that lamps were being collected and prepared for a substantial party of men to go out to search for them. When they explained what they had seen, there was a general celebration, and the drinking began again.

The next day, as the news spread through the city that the phantom was nothing more than cloaked nurses taking a short cut to a side entrance of the hospital building through the cemetery, the people of Thessaloniki settled back with relief into their normal lives. [1]

The unscrupulous and cynical had long used such beliefs for their own purposes. Pashley records an eighteenth-century story narrated to him: "I remember the daughters of a certain miller living next door to me. These two beauties, either through their own machinations or to protect their lovers, used to come to the window in the morning and, pretending to be frightened, exclaim how "two terrifying vampires had entered into the house causing a great disturbance, thrashing around left and right and they grunted and ...they discovered and abducted and tormented us unfortunates all night long." The poor miller, their father, believed in vampires and would lock himself in his room while the daughters did their own thing, not, of course, with skeletons and smallpox vampires but with the two young men "the two night crows," their lovers. It seems that someone, somehow instilled a little courage in the miller who one evening decided to shoot the. ..vampires at the moment when they were leaving. But the miller was not successful except at effecting a breathless stillness. On that evening the miller's two daughters were afraid lest he should summon up his courage and attempt to kill their visitors. [2]

Charles Stewart was told by shepherds in Philoti, Naxos, that thieves told most tales about *xotika* so that people would be unlikely to venture out of doors at night and catch them about their business, and so that if they were seen, they might be mistaken for *xotika* and not followed. [3]

The increasing rarity of *xotika* is sometimes given bizarre explanation. The inhabitants of Sfakia, in Crete, believed that the ravages committed by vampires used, in former times, to be far more frequent than they were when Pashley toured the island, being comparatively rare at that time. This was said to be in consequence of the increased zeal and skill of the clergy in disposing of them. [4]

Xotika were used to explain incomprehensible phenomena. With the development of a scientific world view, better able to explain and control such events, the concept has become useless and irrelevant. Meteorological phenomena such as whirlwinds and water spouts are now explained scientifically. Diseases which formerly were attributed to the attack of *xotika*, and were combated by prayer, holy water and magical charms, and are now attributed to natural causes and combated by medicine: "In the old days people said it was the *Stringlos* who rode on the sheep and caused their death. Today we know it is anthrax that causes it and vaccination which saves us."[5] Moreover, many of the sicknesses and epidemic diseases which they brought, such as smallpox, are happily now eradicated.

Stewart records the following anecdote from Apeiranthos, on Naxos: "the last well-remembered incident involving an *xotiko* centred around a dark figure that roamed the alleyways at night. People thought it was a *stringla* until one evening a brave man challenged her and found that she was just a senile old black-clad woman who had taken to wandering around late at night. Doubt was similarly cast on the woman who claimed to have seen the *Panagia* walking in the village at night. Both this and the incident with the black-clad woman were attributed to the bad lighting on village roads. People said that the car headlights had driven them away."[6] It seems that the *xotika* are on the way to being rationalized out of existence.

Xotika tended to strike people who were in the wrong place at the wrong time, and thus the stories about them functioned as a form of social control. That degree of control over people's movements is no longer enforceable or acceptable: "Now we are the demons and nereids, all of us; we are the *aerika*, In those days people would never think of going out after dark, while now we are all out after midnight, and nobody seems bothered or afraid."[7] Moreover, technological advances and changes in our way of life mean that people no longer go to the well to draw water. They do not spend long hours working at the village threshing floor. They no longer need to go outside in the darkness to urinate. When they travel it is swiftly on in a vehicle, rather than slowly in the darkness on a mule. Thus people do not any more find themselves in those situations where *xotika* were formerly most likely to be encountered.

Yet statements are constantly recorded by researchers which seem to indicate a curious sense that it is not so much that the *xotika* never existed, and that people now realise this, but rather that they have "disappeared," or "gone away." Richard and Eva Blum recorded such statements as: "Generally the *exotica* no longer appear because people have walked on all their places, trod their ground, and there is no room left to them." This sounds like the expression of a vague feeling that something of the mystery has gone out of life, and that in the modern scientific world view we have espoused, there is "no room" for them. It is sometimes said to be the noise of modern life which has driven them away: "In the old days people closed their gates at sunset and opened it only for the following dawn after the rooster had crowed three times. But now, my goodness, there are so many trucks and cars on the road during the night that the exotica are the ones that are afraid, so they do not appear any more."[8]

Today, in modern Athens, the word *vrykolakas* has a new meaning. It is used to refer to a child molester; while a *drakos* is a rapist or strangler.[9]

Such experiences as are not assimilable to the normal tend today to be perceived and described in terms which are consistent with a superficially scientific outlook. In the latter half of the twentieth century, a new generation of modern folk tales emerged, interpreted in terms of UFOs and alien visitations. This began early in the century.

One moonless night at the turn of the century, a shepherd-boy spending the night on Mount Pendeli, outside Athens, looking after his father's sheep, claimed that he saw a large mushroom shaped object, with lights coming from "windows" around it, descend from the skies. When it landed, two individuals "dressed like divers" emerged from a door and approached him. He claimed that, communicating with him directly by thought, they invited him to leave with them. When he refused, they left without him. He rushed into a nearby village and told his story to anyone who would listen.[10]

Since that time, Greece has not been exempt from the UFO and alien sightings which have become common throughout the world, such as the moving lights seen over and over the Saronic Gulf in the area of Porto Heli and Spetses during the autumn of 1992,[11] and over Thessaloniki and the Thermaic Gulf during most of the latter half of the twentieth century,[12] The move from nymph haunted springs to aliens in space suits in flying saucers seems to mark a significant deterioration of taste.

[1] Σεφέρας 103-18.
[2] Κεφαλληνιάδης, Νίκος, Λοιμώδεις ασθένειες στη Νάξο στα περασμένα χρόνια, in Stewart, 112.
[3] Stewart 112.
[4] Pashley 2:202.
[5] Blum & Blum 99.
[6] Stewart 110.
[7] Blum & Blum 54.

[8] Blum & Blum 54.

[9] Stewart 190.

[10] Τσέβα 75.

[11] Νικολούλη.

[12] Σερεφάς 122-31.

Bibliography

ABBOTT, G. F., *Macedonian Folklore,* (Chicago, 1969)

ALEXIOU, Margaret, *The Ritual Lament in Greek Tradition* (Cambridge, 1974)

BENT, James Theodore, *The Cyclades or Life Amongst the Insular Greeks* (London, 1885)

BLUM, Richard & BLUM, Eva, *The Dangerous Hour: The Lore of Crisis and Mystery in Rural Greece* (London, 1970)

CAERNARVON, Earl of, *Reminiscences of Athens and the Morea* (London, 1869)

CARROLL, Michael, *Gates of the Wind* (London, 1965).

DODWELL, Edward, *A Classical and Topographical Tour through Greece in the years 1801, 1805 and 1806* (London, 1819)

DURREL, Lawrence, T*he Greek Islands,* (London, 1978)

EDWARDS, Charles, *Letters from Crete written during the Spring of 1886* (London, 1887)

FERMOR, Patrick Leigh (1) *Mani: Travels in the Southern Peloponnese,* (London, 1958)

FERMOR, Patrick Leigh (2) *Roumeli: Travels in Northern Greece,* (London, 1966)

GRAY, Peter, *People of Poros* (London, 1942)

HALLIDAY, William Reynold, *Greek and Roman Folklore* (London, 1927)

HUGHES, Thomas Smart, *Travels in Sicily, Greece and Albania* (London, 1820)

LAWSON, John Cuthbert, *Modern Greek Folklore and Ancient Greek Religion,* (Cambridge, 1910)

LEE, Dorothy Demetracopoulou. "Greek Accounts of the *Vrykolakas,*" *Journal of American Folklore, 54* (1941) 126-132

MCNALL, Scott G., "The Greek Peasant," *ASA Rose Monograph Series,* American Sociological Association, (Washington, 1974)

MEGAS, George A., *Greek Calendar Customs, 3rd ed.* (Athens, 1982)

MOUSSA, George, *The White Island* (Amsterdam, 1980)

MYRIVILIS, Stratos, *The Mermaid Madonna* Tr. A. Rick (Athens, 1981)

NEWTON, Charles T., *Travels and Discoveries in the Levant* (London, 1865)

PASHLEY, Robert, *Travels in Crete* 2v (Cambridge/London, 1837)

PITTON DE TOURNEFORT, Joseph, *A Voyage into the Levant...* 3v. tr. J. Ozell, D. Midwinter (London, 1741)

RATCLIFFE, Dorothy Una, *Grecian Glory* (London, 1941)

RODD, James Rennell, *The Customs and Lore of Modern Greece*, (London, 1892)

SAPOURIA-SAKELLARAKI, Efi, "The Dragon Houses of Mount Ochi, *Athenian* (Oct. 1989)

SEYMOUR, Thomas D., "Life and Travel in Modern Greece" *Scribner's Magazine* (New York, July 1988), in TOMKINSON (5) 412-4.

SPRATT, Captain T. A. B., *Travels and Researches in Crete* 2v. (London, 1865)

STEWART, Charles. *Demons and the Devil: Moral Imagination in Modern Greek Culture*. Princeton, NJ: Princeton University Press, 1991.

TOMKINSON, John L. (1) *Athens: The City* (Athens, 2002)

TOMKINSON, John L. (2) *Athens: The Suburbs* (Athens, 2002)

TOMKINSON, John L. (3) *Attica The City* (Athens, 2002)

TOMKINSON, John L. (4) *Festive Greece: A Calendar of Tradition* (Athens, 2003)

TOMKINSON John L. (5) *Travellers' Greece: Memories of an Enchanted Land* (Athens, 2002)

WORDSWORTH, Christopher, *Athens and Attica* (London, 1837)

ΑΝΑΓΝΩΣΤΟΠΟΥΛΟΣ, Ιωάννης Σπ., Τα Στοιχειά Αρκουδόβρυσης και Νεραϊδόβρυσης, *Λαογραφικά του Αχλαδόκαμπου* (1985) 114-115.

ΑΥΛΙΔΟΥ, Ευα, Ποιά είναι η Μακεδονία; σε *Μυστική Ελλάδα* 123-168.

ΒΑΟΥ, Ζαφείρη, *Θρύλοι, Μύθοι, Παραδόσεις Προλήψεις Δεισιδαιμονίες της Μήλου* (Χολαργός, 1988)

ΒΟΥΡΝΑΣ, Τάσος και ΓΑΡΙΔΗ, Ελένη, *Η Παράδοση και η επιβίωση της στο σημερινό πολιτισμό μας* (Αθήνα, 1979)

ΓΑΛΛΟΠΟΥΛΟΥ, Λ. κτλ. *Ελληνικός Λαικός Πολιτισμός* (Αθήμα, 1982).

ΓΙΑΝΝΟΠΟΥΛΟΣ, Ιωαννης Θ., Η Μυστική Αθήνα και Αττική Β' εκ. (Αθήνα, 1999)

ΓΙΑΝΝΟΥΛΑΚΗΣ, Παντέλης (1) Η Αλλη Στέρεα Ελλάδα, σε *Μυστική Ελλάδα* 295-307.

ΓΙΑΝΝΟΥΛΑΚΗΣ, Παντέλης, κτλ. (2) *Μυστική Ελλάδα*, (Θεσσαλονίκη, 1999)

ΓΙΑΝΝΟΥΛΑΚΗΣ, Παντέλης (3) Οι Ελληνές Βρυκόλακες, σε *Μυστική Ελλάδα* 375-384.

ΓΙΑΝΝΟΥΛΑΚΗΣ, Παντέλης (4) Το Στοιχειωμένο Σπίτι της Θεσσαλονίκης, σε *Μυστική Ελλάδα* 205-209.

ΔΟΡΜΠΑΡΑΚΗΣ, Παναγιώτης και ΠΑΝΟΥΤΣΟΠΟΥΛΟΥ, Κασσιανή, *Η Περιοχή της Ευρωστίνης Κορινθίας* (Αθήνα, 1992)

ΘΕΟΔΟΣΙΑΔΗΣ, Ν (1), Ο Γυρός της Αχρονης Πελοποννήσου, σε *Μυστική Ελλάδα* 339-373.

ΘΕΟΔΟΣΙΑΔΗΣ, Ν, Τα Ελληνικά Ξωτικά, σε *Μυστική Ελλάδα* 79-86.

ΘΕΟΔΟΣΙΑΔΗΣ, Ν (3) Για των Ταξιδιωτητων Επτά Νησιων, σε *Μυστική Ελλάδα* 467-85.

ΘΕΟΔΟΣΙΑΔΗΣ, Ν (4) Ξωτικά Γ' εκ. (Θεσσαλονίκι, 2003)

ΚΑΚΟΥΡΗ, Κατερίνας Ι., Θανατος – αναστάσεις σε μαγικό-θρησκεύτικα «δρώμενα» της λαϊκής λατρειας της Ήπειρου, *Βιβλιωθήκη Ηπειρωτικης Εταιρείας, 9* (Αθήνα, 1965)

ΚΑΜΗΛΑΚΗ, Αικατερίνης, Μύθοι και λαϊκές παραδόσεις, *Καθημερινή Επτά Ημέρες* (15.07.01)

ΚΑΜΠΟΥΡΟΓΛΟΥ, Δ. Γρ. (1) *Αι Παλαίαι Αθήναι*, (Αθήνα, 1922)

ΚΑΜΠΟΥΡΟΓΛΟΥ, Δ. Γρ. (2) Ο Αναδρομάρης της Αττικής (Αθήνα, 1920)

172

ΚΑΝΑΚΑΡΗΣ, Νίκος (1) Η Μυστική Σύρος, σε *Μυστική Ελλάδα* 431-445.

ΚΑΝΑΚΑΡΗΣ, Νίκος (2) Ταξίδι στις Αγνώστες Κυκλάδες, σε *Μυστική Ελλάδα* 397-415.

ΚΑΡΑΣΟΥΤΑΣ, Θεόδωρος, Λαικός πολιτισμός: Κλειτορολευκασιας καλαβρυτων, (Αθήνα, 1999)

ΚΕΦΑΛΛΗΝΙΑΔΗΣ, Νίκος Α., *Τα Σπήλαια της Νάξου και οι θρύλοι των* (Αθήνα, 1961)

ΚΟΥΝΕΝΑΚΗ, Πέγκυ, Γοργόνα, η μυθική αδελφή του Μαεγαέξανδρου, *Καθημερινή Επτά Ημέρες* (15.07.01)

ΚΥΡΙΑΚΙΔΟΥ-ΝΕΣΤΟΡΟΣ, Άλκι, Συμάδια του τόπου ή η λιγική του Ελληνικού τοπίου, *Λαογραφικά Μελετήματα* (1975).

ΚΩΣΤΑΚΗΣ, Θαν. Π., Θεότητες και δαιμονικά Τσακωνιάς *Λαογραφία* 33 (1982-84) –92

ΛΟΥΚΑΤΟΣ, Δημήτριος. Σ., Το Δωδεκαήμερο και οι τρεις Γιορτές του στην Κεφαλονιά, *Επτανήσιο Ημερολόγιο* (1960)

ΜΑΝΤΖΟΥΡΑΝΗ, Επ. Γ., Κυνουριακαί Παραδόσεις, *Λαογραφία Δ'* (1913-4) 464-75.

ΜΟΛΙΝΟΣ, Στρατής Αλ., Θρύλων των Κάστρων Μας, (Αθήνα, 1995)

ΝΙΚΟΛΟΥΛΗ, Αγγελική, "Είδαμε UFO στις Σπέτσες" *Εθνος της Κυριακής*, 13.12.99.

ΝΟΥΑΡΟΥ, Μιχαήλ Γ. Μιχαηλίδου, *Λαογραφία Σύμμειϰτα Κάρπαθου, Β' εκ.* (Αθήνα, 1969)

ΟΡΦΑΝΟΥΔΑΚΗΣ, Ν., Δροσούλιτες, *Μυστική Ελλάδα* 501-506.

ΠΕΡΔΙΚΑ, Νίκη Λ., Σκύρος: *Μνημεία του λόγου του λαού, 2 τομ.* (Αθήνα, 1943)

ΠΟΛΙΤΗΣ, Νικόλαος, *Παραδόσεις*, 2τ, (Αθήνα, 1994)

ΣΕΡΕΦΑΣ, Σάκης, Πτώματα και Φαντάσματα στη Θεσσαλονίκη του εμφυλίου (Αθήνα, 1998)

ΣΕΡΑΦΕΙΜ, Κώστας Δ., *Λαογραφικά της Αργολίδος*, (Αθήνα, 1981)

ΣΤΑΜΑΤΟΥΛΗ, Ι.Π., Το Στοιχειό τπυ Γουύρα, *Λαογραφία Γ'* (1911-2) 669-671.

ΣΤΑΜΚΟΣ, Γιώργος, Η Αγνωστη Θράκη, σε *Μυστική Ελλάδα*, 19-52.

ΣΤΑΜΠΟΥΉΣ, Γ., Η ζωή των Θεσσαλονικέων πριν και μετά 1912 (Διόσκουροι, 1984)

ΤΣΕΒΑ, Αγγελικής, Λαογράφικα Παραλειπομενα από την Πεντέλη και από τις γυρώ περιοχές, *Ιστορία, Θρύλοι και Παραδόσεις του Πεντέλικου Βουνού, Εξωραιστικός- Επιμορφωτικός Σύλλογος της Πεντέλης* (Αθήνα, 1983)

ΤΣΙΚΛΙΔΗΣ, Μενέλαος Γ. (1) *Αττική η Μαγική Γη*, 2τ (1998, 1999)

ΤΣΙΚΛΙΔΗΣ, Μενέλαος Γ. (2) *Η Αγνωστη Πελοπόννησος* 2τ (Αθήνα, 2000, 2001)

ΤΣΟΥΓΚΑΣ, Χρήστος Κ., *Κρυμμένοι Θησαυροί Στην Ελλάδα*, (Αθήνα, 1996)

ΧΑΤΖΗΔΑΚΗ, Γιωργίου, Η Γοργόνα και το παρελθόν της, *Καθημερινη Επτα Ημερες* (15.07.01)

If you enjoyed this book, you might like to read other books from Anagnosis about Greece by John L. Tomkinson

Travellers' Greece:
Memories of an Enchanted Land
608 pages - Illustrated
ISBN 960-87186-4-3
More than one hundred writers record their impressions of Greece over three centuries.

"[The compiler] has trawled the treasure trove of writings by visitors who travelled in Greece in earlier days ... whatever their source, these excerpts say as much about their authors and their backgrounds as they do about Greece." *Kathimerini* (English Edition)

Festive Greece:
A Calendar of Tradition
144 pages - Illustrated in colour
ISBN 960-87186-7-8
A unique calendar of folk, religious, military and historical festivals, with their origins and background

"[F]or someone wanting to know where to go, and more particularly, when, this is the book for them." *Kathimerini* (English Edition)

Between Heaven and Earth:
The Greek Church
160 pages - Illustrated in colour
ISBN 960-87186-5-1
An account of the history, faith, worship, institutions, and customs of the oldest Christian Church in Europe

GREECE BEYOND THE GUIDEBOOKS

"They are the kind of books that may remind you of your favorite history teacher, the one who told you the interesting and strange pieces of history that the text books left out. From close encounters of the third kind to little-known temples, haunted villas, secret schools and teachings and even stories of Jesus walking in Attika in the 1930's."   Matt Barrett, in *Matt Barrett's Greece Travel Guides*

Athens: The City
160 pages - Illustrated
ISBN 960-87186-0-0
Stories from the history and folklore of the historic and modern city centre of Athens

Athens: The Suburbs
160 pages - Illustrated
ISBN 960-87186-1-9
Stories from the history and folklore of the suburbs of Athens, between the mountains and the sea

Attica
160 pages - Illustrated
ISBN 960-87186-2-7
Stories from the history and folklore of mainland Attica

"As old, richly complex folklore elements become crudely oversimplified and the commercialized, plastic modern world tightens its hold, one needs to grab as many of these books as possible."   *Kathimerini* (English Edition)

For up to date information about Anagnosis books
visit our website: **www.anagnosis.gr**
email: anagnosis@anagnosis.gr

Anagnosis, Harilaou Trikoupi 130, Kifissia 14563 Greece
fax: ++30-210-62-54-089
telephone: ++30-210-62-54-654